Voices of South Asia

Voices of South Asia

Essential Readings from Antiquity to the Present

Patrick Peebles, Editor

LONDON AND NEW YORK

Dedicated to Lynn H. Nelson—mentor, colleague, and friend.

First published 2012 by M.E. Sharpe

Published 2015 by Routledge
2 Park Square, Milton Park, Abingdon, Oxon OX14 4RN
711 Third Avenue, New York, NY 10017, USA

Routledge is an imprint of the Taylor & Francis Group, an informa business

Library of Congress Cataloging-in-Publication Data

Voices of South Asia : essential readings from antiquity to the present / edited by Patrick Peebles.
p. cm.
Includes bibliographical references.
ISBN 978-0-7656-3480-1 (hardcover : alk. paper)—ISBN 978-0-7656-2072-9 (pbk.)
1. India—Civilization—Sources. I. Peebles, Patrick.

DS423.V65 2012
954—dc23 2011038442

ISBN 13: 9780765620729 (pbk)
ISBN 13: 9780765634801 (hbk)

Contents

Preface

Interest in Asian civilizations has grown rapidly throughout the United States over the past several decades and is reflected by the expanding integration of the Asian heritage into our school curriculum. Many colleges and universities now feature strong departments related to specific Asian regions and cultures, including South Asia, East Asia, and Southeast Asia. Numerous resources, both in print and online, are available for the study of these cultures, but many are not easily accessed and many that are do not have the necessary explanations to make these materials relevant to the interested student and general reader.

Voices of South Asia: Essentials Readings from Antiquity to the Present is the first of three titles devoted to three major Asian regions. Over the next several years, M.E. Sharpe will publish *Voices of East Asia: Essential Readings and Images from China, Japan, and Korea* and *Voices of Southeast Asia: Essential Readings from Antiquity to the Present.* The overall purpose of these books is, first, to make great source readings accessible to a wide reading audience and, second, to enhance the reader's understanding of the importance of these works for both the era in which they were written and the relevance that they still hold for us today.

The twenty source readings that make up this volume have been drawn from a wide variety of genres in order to illustrate the richness and diversity of the South Asian heritage. They represent a fair selection of South Asia's ancient and modern classics of thought and expression; and they constitute a unique combination of poetry, novels, short stories, and political and philosophical treatises.

In order to provide a degree of unity to what otherwise might be a simple assortment of excerpts of well-known works, a measure of selectivity and a means of discrimination are necessary. In making these choices, the intention has been to address important issues that are common to all cultures and time periods in South Asia and central to South Asian thought and values. These particular themes include love, death, war and peace, honor, individualism and social obligation, culture and change, and the relationship between thought and action. The hope is that these selections will allow the reader not only to appreciate South Asian traditions, but also to relate these traditions to familiar and significant issues in Western culture.

The work has been structured and sufficient background and explanatory material included in order to provide maximum adaptability—in South Asian and world history courses, in humanities, and in South Asian literature and comparative literature courses. Although not all of the twenty readings are complete works, the attempt has been made to ensure that the material presented is both substantial and representative.

Each selection is prefaced by a detailed essay that discusses its specific historical context, the author, and the work. A set of questions at the beginning of each selection directs the student's attention to major issues within the reading.

This apparatus and structure enable instructor, student, and general reader to utilize the work at a number of levels and for a variety of functions. Readings might be assigned simply as supplemental to and illustrative of the material presented by a core textbook, or course activities could be organized around the readings themselves. One or more selections might serve as the starting point of a paper. The discussion questions raise issues suitable for student papers and discussions or can serve as themes around which the instructor might wish to center classroom presentations. Finally, the reader should simply enjoy the richness and beauty of some of the greatest writings from South Asia.

I wish to acknowledge the valuable assistance and counsel that I have received from Steven Drummond at M.E. Sharpe Publishers in the conception and preparation of this volume. In addition, I have enjoyed the full support of the editorial staff at M.E. Sharpe and wish to extend my particular thanks to Kimberly Giambattisto.

I would also like to express my appreciation to the following individuals for their advice and suggestions in both the selection and preparation of the accompanying apparatus: Ed Bushey of Johnson County Community College and Susanne Mitko of Avila College. Also, Jean Arasanayagam has kindly given permission to use her work *All Is Burning* and provided comment in the accompanying essay.

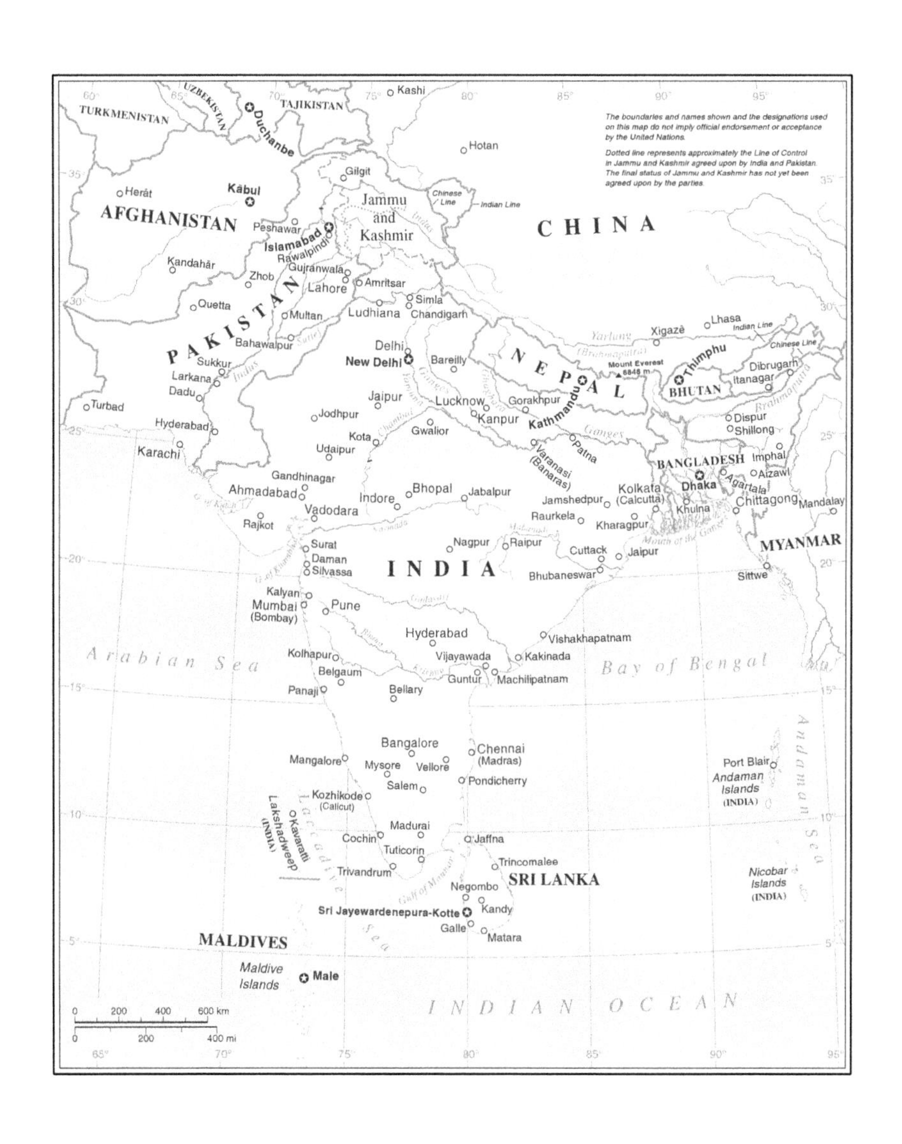

Map of South Asia

Voices of South Asia

✧ Vedic Hymns ✧

Some time after 1500 BCE the center of civilization in South Asia shifted from the ancient urban society centered on the valley of the Indus river to one led by migrants speaking Indo-European languages. Once thought to be a conquering horde of warriors—a misperception that fueled the racist fantasies of Hitler and others—these migrants, known as Aryans, probably arrived over a period of centuries as a pastoral and nomadic people on the fringes of the great cities. They brought the Sanskrit language, a pantheon of deities, and a ritualistic cult based on sacrificial fire and an intoxicating drink called *soma*. The Aryans valued cattle as their primary source of wealth, and the importance of these animals to the conquerors was perhaps the origin of the later Hindu reverence for the cow.

The Aryans were organized into patriarchal tribes that were in turn composed of hereditary classes, called *varna*. The Aryans themselves formed the noble class, divided into the warriors (*Rajanya* or *Kshatriya*) and the priests (*Brahman*). Commoners (*Vaisya*) filled all the other respectable occupations. They regarded the bulk of the non-Aryan population as serfs (*Sudra*) or slaves. These four classes survived long after Aryan society disappeared. The "Book of Man" gives a religious sanction for these categories. Over time a fifth category emerged of people so low in status that they did not belong to any category. Such people were called in English "untouchables," since the other *varnas* felt defiled by merely touching them.

Early Aryan religion was designed to placate the natural and supernatural forces that influenced human life; it was simple and straightforward, attributing unexplainable events as well as natural phenomena—thunder, lightning, rain, and the fertility of the soil—to the actions of the Aryan gods. These gods favored the Aryans when the priests performed sacrifices regularly and correctly. The magical power of the sacrifice to persuade the gods to do what humans wanted them to do was called *brahman*, from which the name of the priestly class derived. The Brahmans were not only the priests of the Aryans, but also their wise men, preserving traditions, laws, and—most of all—knowledge of the gods and their ways for future generations. The Brahmans transmitted this knowledge orally for hundreds of years almost perfectly unchanged, until they were able to write it down. One of the earliest collections of Aryan lore is that known as the Vedas, composed of hymns, prayers, and songs that are now considered sacred by Hindus. The hymns of the *Rig Veda* are the earliest Vedic texts, composed between 1500 and 1200 BCE.

The Vedas preserve songs of homage to the deities, myths, formulas for rituals and sacrifices, and philosophical speculation. Some of the deities to whom these hymns are addressed have their counterparts in the pantheons of other Indo-European peoples, especially those of Iran, Greece, and Rome, suggesting a common origin in prehistoric times for all of these religions. For example, Dyaus Pitar, the "Sky Father" in the Vedas, is clearly cognate with Zeus Pater in Greek and Jupiter in Latin. Varuna may be identified with Uranus.

Many of the hymns of the *Rig Veda* glorify the martial character of the Aryans. Indra, originally a rain god associated with thunder, was later associated with the destruction of the citadels, dams, and irrigation works of the Indus Valley civilization. As the Aryans settled in the land of the five rivers, or Punjab, and extended their conquests into the Ganges plain, Indra began to assume a central role among their other gods. The Aryan pantheon continued to evolve, and the belief system grew more complex. Vishnu, who is a minor deity mentioned in the *Rig Veda* only in the hymn given here, later became perhaps the greatest of the Hindu gods. Varuna is the god of sky and the oceans and evolved into the lord of heaven and earth. The idea of transmigration, or the cycle of rebirth, is not mentioned in the earliest sacred texts that have survived; like other Indo-European peoples, the Aryans appear to have believed in a kind of paradise in which the gods dwelled and in a hell ruled by the god Yama, who tortured wicked souls after death. Only later did they develop the belief that souls did not go to an afterlife, but instead returned to another life in a continuous cycle of rebirth and death.

Questions

1. How do the hymns "To Night" and "To Dawn" view nature?
2. In the hymns, what evidence is given of the Aryan transition from pastoral nomadism to settled agriculture?
3. What can we learn about the daily lives, values, and material culture of the Aryans by reading these hymns?
4. "Creation" and the "Book of Man" are dated to a later period on the basis of linguistic evidence. Do they show evidence of the evolution of Indian religious thought?

Vedic Hymns

Ralph T.H. Griffith, trans., *Hymns of the Rigveda*
(Benares: E.J. Lazarus, 1897)

To Visnu

I will declare the mighty deeds of Visnu, of him who measured out the earthly regions,
Who propped the highest place of congregation, thrice setting down his footstep, widely striding.

For this his mighty deed is Visnu lauded, like some wild beast, dread, prowling, mountain roaming;
He within whose three wide-extended paces all living creatures have their habitation.

Let the hymn lift itself as strength to Visnu, the Bull, far-striding, dwelling on the mountains,
Him who alone with triple step hath measured this common dwelling-place, long, far extended,

Him whose three places that are filled with sweetness, imperishable, joy as it may list them,
Who verily alone upholds the threefold, the earth, the heaven, and all living creatures.

May I attain to that his well-loved mansion where men devoted to the gods are happy.

For there springs, close akin to the wide-strider, the well of meath[1] in Visnu's highest footstep.
Fain would we go unto your dwelling-places where there are many horned and nimble oxen,
For mightily, there, shineth down upon us the widely-striding Bull's sublimest mansion.

Book 1, Hymn 154

To Varuna

Sing forth a hymn sublime and solemn, grateful to glorious Varuna, imperial ruler,
Who hath struck out, like one who slays the victim, earth as a skin to spread in front of the sun.

In the tree-tops the air he hath extended, put milk in kine[2] and vigorous speed in horses,
Set intellect in hearts, fire in the waters, the sun in heaven and Soma on the mountain.

Varuna lets the big cask, opening downward, flow through the heaven and earth and air's mid-region.
Therewith the universe's sovereign waters earth as the shower of rain bedews the barley.

When Varuna is fain for milk, he moistens the sky, the land, and earth to her foundation.
Then straight the mountains clothe them in the rain-cloud: the heroes, putting forth their vigour, loose them.

I will declare this mighty deed of magic, of glorious Varuna, the lord immortal,
Who, standing in the firmament, hath meted the earth out with the sun as with a measure.

None, verily, hath ever let or hindered this the most wise god's mighty deed of magic,
Whereby with all their flood, the lucid rivers fill not one sea wherein they pour their waters.

---

[1] Intoxicating liquor.
[2] Cows.

If we have sinned against the man who loves us, have ever wronged a brother, friend, or comrade,
The neighbour ever with us, or a stranger, O Varuna, remove from us the trespass.

If we, as gamesters cheat at play, have cheated, done wrong unwittingly or sinned of purpose,
Cast all these sins away like loosened fetters, and, Varuna, let us be thine own beloved.

Book 5, Hymn 85

To Dawn

She hath shone brightly like a youthful woman, stirring to motion every living creature.
Agni[3] hath come to feed on mortals' fuel. She hath made light and chased away the darkness.

Turned to this all, far-spreading, she hath risen and shone in brightness with white robes about her.
She hath beamed forth lovely with golden colours, mother of kine, guide of the days she bringeth.

Bearing the gods' own eye, auspicious lady, leading her courser white and fair to look on,
Distinguished by her beams, Dawn shines apparent, come forth to all the world with wondrous treasure.

Draw nigh with wealth and dawn away the foeman: prepare for us wide pasture free from danger.
Drive away those who hate us, bring us riches: pour bounty, opulent lady, on the singer.

Send thy most excellent beams to shine and light us, giving us lengthened days, O Dawn, O goddess,
Granting us food, thou who hast all things precious, and bounty rich in chariots, kine, and horses.

O Dawn, nobly-born, daughter of heaven, whom the Vasisthas[4] with their hymns make mighty,

[3] God of fire.
[4] Poet seers.

Bestow thou on us vast and glorious riches. Preserve us evermore, ye gods, with blessings.

Book 7, Hymn 77

To Night

With all her eyes the goddess Night looks forth approaching many a spot:
She hath put all her glories on.

Immortal, she hath filled the waste, the goddess hath filled height and depth:
She conquers darkness with her light.

The goddess as she comes hath set the Dawn her sister in her place:
And then the darkness vanishes.

So favour us this night, O thou whose pathways we have visited
As birds their nest upon the tree.

The villagers have sought their homes, and all that walks and all that flies,
Even the falcons fain for prey.

Keep off the she-wolf and the wolf; O Night, keep the thief away:
Easy be thou for us to pass.

Clearly hath she come nigh to me who decks the dark with richest hues:
O morning, cancel it like debts.

These have I brought to thee like kine. O Night, thou child of heaven, accept
This laud as for a conqueror.

Book 10, Hymn 127

The Book of Man

A thousand heads hath Purusa,[5] a thousand eyes, a thousand feet.
On every side pervading earth he fills a space ten fingers wide.

This Purusa is all that yet hath been and all that is to be,
The lord of immortality which waxes greater still by food.

So mighty is his greatness; yea, greater than this is Purusa.
All creatures are one-fourth of him, three-fourths eternal life in heaven.

With three-fourths Purusa went up; one-fourth of him again was here.
Thence he strode out to every side over what eats not and what eats.

From him Viraj[6] was born; again Purusa from Viraj was born.
As soon as he was born he spread eastward and westward o'er the earth.

When gods prepared the Sacrifice with Purusa as their offering,
Its oil was spring; the holy gift was autumn; summer was the wood.

They balmed as victim on the grass Purusa born in earliest time.
With him the deities and all Sadhyas[7] and Rsis[8] sacrificed.

From that great general Sacrifice the dripping fat was gathered up.
He formed the creatures of the air, and animals both wild and tame.

From that great general Sacrifice Rcs[9] and Sama-hymns[10] were born;

---

[5] Primeval being.
[6] The material universe.
[7] Celestial beings.
[8] Ancient seers.
[9] Verses.
[10] Hymns of the *Sama Veda*; meant to be chanted.

Therefrom were spells and charms produced; the Yajus[11] had their birth from it.

From it were horses born, from it all cattle with two rows of teeth:
From it were gathered kine, from it the goats and sheep were born.

When they divided Purusa, how many portions did they make?
What do they call his mouth, his arms? What do they call his thighs and feet?

The Brahman was his mouth, of both his arms was the Rajanya made.
His thighs became the Vaisya, from his feet the Sudra was produced.

The moon was gendered from his mind, and from his eye the sun had birth;
Indra and Agni from his mouth were born and Vayu[12] from his breath.

Forth from his navel came mid-air; the sky was fashioned from his head;
Earth from his feet, and from his ear the regions. Thus they formed the worlds.

Seven fencing-sticks had he, thrice seven layers of fuel were prepared,
When the gods, offering sacrifice, bound, as their victim, Purusa.

Gods, sacrificing, sacrificed the victim: these were the earliest holy ordinance.
The mighty ones attained the height of heaven, there where the Sadhyas, gods of old, are dwelling.

Book 10, Hymn 90

[11] Hymns of the *Yaju-Veda*; sung at sacrifices.
[12] God of wind.

Creation

Then was not non-existent nor existent: there was no realm of air, no sky beyond it.
What covered in, and where? and what gave shelter? Was water there, unfathomed depth of water?

Death was not then, nor was there aught immortal: no sign was there, the day's and night's divider.
That one thing, breathless, breathed by its own nature: apart from it was nothing whatsoever.

Darkness there was: at first concealed in darkness, this All was indiscriminated chaos.
All that existed then was void and formless: by the great power of warmth was born that unit.

Thereafter rose desire in the beginning, Desire, the primal seed and germ of spirit.
Sages who searched with their heart's thought discovered the existent's kinship in the non-existent.

Transversely was their severing line extended: what was above it then, and what below it?
There were begetters, there were mighty forces, free action here and energy up yonder.

Who verily knows and who can here declare it, whence it was born and whence came this creation?
The gods are later than this world's production. Who knows, then, whence it first came into being?
He, the first origin of this creation, whether he formed it all or did not form it,
Whose eye controls this world in highest heaven, he verily knows it, or perhaps he knows not.

Book 10, Hymn 126

✧ Sermon at the Deer Park ✧

Siddhartha Gautama Buddha

Karma (one's actions) and *samsara* (transmigration, the results of one's actions) are the nearest things to religious dogma in Hinduism. By the sixth century BCE, the concept of *karma* increasingly came to mean ritually prescribed behavior—that is, fulfilling religious obligations rather than performing good deeds. This change enhanced the role of the Brahmans, since they were the only caste allowed to perform sacrifices, and other castes had to turn to them for assistance in fulfilling their religious debts. It was believed that Brahmans' sacrifices had the magical power to compel the gods to respond to human prayers. At the same time, individual duty (*dharma*) ceased being interpreted in broad human terms and increasingly came to be defined in terms of caste occupation. In this way, the individual was removed from the center of religious activity in favor of the Brahmans, and individual morality tended to become merely a means of reinforcing a stratified and unequal social system.

Religious reformers appeared in India in the middle of the first millennium BCE. Among their contributions to Hinduism are a series of commentaries on, and explanations of, the Vedas. The most important of these are called Upanishads, some of which were written about 550 BCE. The Upanishads speculate on the mechanics of transmigration, concluding that *karma* determines how one is reborn. If one's deeds are good, the soul (*atman*) is reborn into a higher status; if they are evil, one will live one's next lifetime in a lower status. The Upanishads combined the concept of *brahman* mentioned in the Vedic sacrifices with the *atman* or soul that transmigrates. The *brahman* was the "universal soul," and salvation meant the reunification of the *atman* with *brahman*.

Other reformers rejected the authority of the Vedas with their emphasis on sacrifice and the inequality between classes and their neglect of personal moral responsibilities. Much of this heterodox thought appears to have come from tribal kingdoms on the fringes of the Ganges plain that had only recently and incompletely absorbed Aryan social institutions. One such kingdom, that of the Sakyas, lying in the foothills of the Himalayas, gave birth to the greatest challenger of Hindu orthodoxy, the founder of Buddhism, Gautama Siddhartha (480–400 BCE?).

The goal of religious effort in the Buddha's teachings was enlightenment (*nirvana*)—a release from the constant cycle of birth and rebirth and a cessation of any consciousness of self. He distinguished this from the Upanishads' view that salvation consists of the merging of individual and universal souls by explicitly denying the existence of the soul, and he explained transmigration as merely the movement of a life-force, like a flame passing from candle to candle. He also denied that the Brahmans had any special status or peculiar power in the cosmic order. In this sense, he founded a democratic and personal religion in which each individual was to seek personal enlightenment.

The biography of the "historical Buddha" is an important part of Buddhist beliefs, particularly for Theravada Buddhists, for whom he is a model of the path of renunciation and moderation that leads to enlightenment. Siddhartha is believed to have left his protected and pampered life in his father's court at the age of twenty-nine to become an ascetic. He practiced various systems of self-mortification and remained for six years with the five ascetics mentioned in this selection, practicing asceticism in an effort to understand the meaning of things and the path to enlightenment. Although he increased his psychic powers considerably, he decided that this alone had not brought him any closer to enlightenment. It had, in fact, prevented him from maintaining the inner calm necessary for successful meditation. The ascetics left him in disgust when he abandoned his extreme practices. He then meditated alone under the Tree of Wisdom at Gaya and repulsed temptation from the demon Mara. The following selection describes his enlightenment and first actions as conceived by the sect of saffron-robed mendicants (*bhikshus*) who followed his teachings in later centuries. He discovered the "Four Noble Truths" and became a *buddha*, or "enlightened one," and returned to Benares, where he sought the five ascetics, who became his disciples. According to later texts, he preached the following sermon, in which he set out the basic principles of his teachings, in the Deer Park outside the city. The Buddha chose not to pass into the state of *nirvana*, but remained on earth for forty more years, teaching and attracting disciples.

There are no images of the Buddha for centuries after his lifetime; however, there are some interesting examples of the symbol used to represent the Buddha at http://viewonbuddhism.org/general_symbols_buddhism.html.

Questions

1. Why does the Buddha say that ignorance is the root of all evil?
2. How did the five ascetics greet the Buddha? Why?
3. What is the "middle path"? Why does the Buddha consider it better spiritually than asceticism?
4. From this reading, would you say that the Buddha's teaching constituted a religion, or was it moral philosophy?

Sermon at the Deer Park

Paul Carus, *The Gospel of Buddha, According to Old Records*, 4th revised ed. (Chicago: Open Court Publishing, 1896), pp. 30–33, 37–43

Bodhisattva having put to flight Mara, gave himself up to meditation. All the miseries of the world, the evils produced by evil deeds and the sufferings arising therefrom passed before his mental eye, and he thought:

"Surely if living creatures saw the results of all their evil deeds, they would turn away from them in disgust. But selfhood blinds them, and they cling to their obnoxious desires.

"They crave for pleasure and they cause pain; when death destroys their individuality, they find no peace; their thirst for existence abides and their selfhood reappears in new births.

"Thus they continue to move in the coil and can find no escape from the hell of their own making. And how empty are their pleasures, how vain are their endeavors! Hollow like the plantain-tree and without contents like the bubble.

"The world is full of sin and sorrow, because it is full of error. Men go astray because they think that delusion is better than truth. Rather than truth they follow error, which is pleasant to look at in the beginning but causes anxiety, tribulation, and misery."

And Bodhisattva began to expound the dharma. The dharma is the truth. The dharma is the sacred law. The dharma is religion. The dharma alone can deliver us from error, sin, and sorrow.

Pondering on the origin of birth and death, the Enlightened One recognised that ignorance was the root of all evil; and these are the links in the development of life, called the twelve *nidanas:*

"In the beginning there is existence blind and without knowledge; and in this sea of ignorance there are appetences formative and organising. From appetences, formative and organising, rises awareness or feelings. Feelings beget organisms that live as individual beings. These organisms develop the six fields, that is, the five senses and the mind. The six fields come in contact with things. Contact begets sensation. Sensation creates the thirst of individualised being. The thirst of being creates a cleaving to things. The cleaving produces the growth and continuation of selfhood. Selfhood continues in renewed births. The renewed births of selfhood are the cause of suffering, old age, sickness, and death. They produce lamentation, anxiety, and despair.

"The cause of all sorrow lies at the very beginning; it is hidden in the ignorance from which life grows. Remove ignorance and you will destroy the wrong appetences that rise from ignorance; destroy these appetences and you will wipe out the wrong perception that rises from them. Destroy wrong perception and there is an end of errors in individualised beings. Destroy errors in individualised beings and the illusions of the six fields will disappear. Destroy illusions and the contact with things will cease to beget misconception. Destroy misconception and you do away with thirst. Destroy thirst and you will be free of all morbid cleaving. Remove the cleaving and you destroy the selfishness of selfhood. If the selfishness of selfhood is destroyed you will be above birth, old age, disease, and death, and you escape all suffering."

The Enlightened One saw the four noble truths which point out the path that leads to Nirvana or the extinction of self:

"The first noble truth is the existence of sorrow. Birth is sorrowful, growth is sorrowful, illness is sorrowful, and death is sorrowful. Sad it is to be joined with that which we do not like. Sadder still is the separation from that which we love, and painful is the craving for that which cannot be obtained.

"The second noble truth is the cause of suffering. The cause of suffering is lust. The surrounding world affects sensation and begets a craving thirst, which clamors for immediate satisfaction. The illusion of self originates and manifests itself in a cleaving to things. The desire to live for the enjoyment of self entangles us in the net of sorrow. Pleasures are the bait and the result is pain.

"The third noble truth is the cessation of sorrow. He who conquers self will be free from lust. He no longer craves, and the flame of desire finds no material to feed upon. Thus it will be extinguished.

"The fourth noble truth is the eightfold path that leads to the cessation of sorrow. There is salvation for him whose self disappears before Truth, whose will is bent upon what he ought to do, whose sole desire is the performance of his duty. He who is wise will enter this path and make an end of sorrow. The eightfold path is (1) right comprehension; (2) right resolutions; (3) right speech; (4) right acts; (5) right way of earning a livelihood; (6) right efforts; (7) right thoughts; and (8) the right state of a peaceful mind." This is the dharma. This is the truth.

Now the Blessed One thought: "To whom shall I preach the doctrine first? My old teachers are dead. They would have received the good news with joy. But my five disciples are still alive. I shall go to them, and to them shall I first proclaim the gospel of deliverance."

At that time the five *bhikshus* dwelt in the Deer Park at Benares, and the Blessed One not thinking of their unkindness in having left him at a time when he was most in need of their sympathy and help, but mindful only of the services which they had ministered unto him, and pitying them for the austerities which they practised in vain, rose and journeyed to their abode.

The five *bhikshus* saw their old teacher approach and agreed among themselves not to salute him, nor to address him as a master, but by his name only. "For," so they said, "he has broken his vow and has abandoned holiness. He is no *bhikshu* but Gautama, and Gautama has become a man who lives in abundance and indulges in the pleasures of worldliness."

But when the Blessed One approached in a dignified manner, they involuntarily rose from their seats and greeted him in spite of their resolution. Still they called him by his name and addressed him as "friend."

When they had thus received the Blessed One, he said: "Do not call the Tathagata[1] by his name nor address him 'friend,' for he is Buddha, the Holy One. Buddha looks equally with a kind heart on all living beings and they therefore call him 'Father.' To disrespect a father is wrong; to despise him, is sin.

"The Tathagata," Buddha continued, "does not seek salvation in austerities, but for that reason you must not think that he indulges in worldly pleasures, nor does he live in abundance. The Tathagata has found the middle path.

"Neither abstinence from fish or flesh, nor going naked, nor shaving the head, nor wearing matted hair, nor dressing in a rough garment, nor covering oneself with dirt, nor sacrificing to Agni, will cleanse a man who is not free from delusions.

"Reading the Vedas, making offerings to priests, or sacrifices to the gods, self-mortification by heat or cold, and many such penances performed for the sake of immortality, these do not cleanse the man who is not free from delusions.

"Anger, drunkenness, obstinacy, bigotry, deception, envy, self-praise, disparaging others, superciliousness, and evil intentions constitute uncleanness; not verily the eating of flesh.

"Let me teach you, O *bhikshus*, the middle path, which keeps aloof from both extremes. By suffering, the emaciated devotee produces confusion and sickly thoughts in his mind. Mortification is not conducive even to worldly knowledge; how much less to a triumph over the senses!

"He who fills his lamp with water will not dispel the darkness, and he who tries to light a fire with rotten wood will fail.

"Mortifications are painful, vain, and profitless. And how can any one be free from self by leading a wretched life if he does not succeed in quenching the fires of lust.

"All mortification is vain so long as self remains, so long as self continues to lust after either worldly or heavenly pleasures. But he in whom self has become extinct is free from lust; he will desire neither worldly nor heavenly pleasures, and the satisfaction of his natural wants will not defile him. Let him eat and drink according to the needs of the body.

"Water surrounds the lotus-flower, but does not wet its petals.

"On the other hand, sensuality of all kind is enervating. The sensual man is a slave of his passions, and pleasure-seeking is degrading and vulgar.

---

[1] "One who has found the truth"—the name Buddha uses to refer to himself.

"But to satisfy the necessities of life is not evil. To keep the body in good health is a duty, for otherwise we shall not be able to trim the lamp of wisdom, and keep our mind strong and clear.

"This is the middle path, O *bhikshus*, that keeps aloof from both extremes."

And the Blessed One spoke kindly to his disciples, pitying them for their errors, and pointing out the uselessness of their endeavors, and the ice of ill-will that chilled their hearts melted away under the gentle warmth of the Master's persuasion. Now the Blessed One set the wheel of the most excellent law a-rolling, and he began to preach to the five *bhikshus*, opening to them the gate of immortality, and showing them the bliss of Nirvana.

And when the Blessed One began his sermon, a rapture thrilled through all the universes.

The *devas* left their heavenly abodes to listen to the sweetness of the truth; the saints that had parted from life crowded around the great teacher to receive the glad tidings; even the animals of the earth felt the bliss that rested upon the words of the Tathagata: and all the creatures of the host of sentient beings, gods, men, and beasts, hearing the message of deliverance, received and understood it in their own language.

Buddha said:

"The spokes of the wheel are the rules of pure conduct; justice is the uniformity of their length; wisdom is the tire; modesty and thoughtfulness are the hub in which the immovable axle of truth is fixed.

"He who recognises the existence of suffering, its cause, its remedy, and its cessation has fathomed the four noble truths. He will walk in the right path.

"Right views will be the torch to light his way. Right aims will be his guide. Right words will be his dwelling-place on the road. His gait will be straight, for it is right behavior. His refreshments will be the right way of earning his livelihood. Right efforts will be his steps: right thoughts his breath; and peace will follow in his footprints."

And the Blessed One explained the instability of the ego.

"Whatsoever is originated will be dissolved again. All worry about the self is vain; the ego is like a mirage, and all the tribulations that touch it will pass away. They will vanish like a nightmare when the sleeper awakes.

"He who has awakened is freed from fear; he has become Buddha; he knows the vanity of all his cares, his ambitions, and also of his pains.

"It easily happens that a man, when taking a bath, steps upon a wet rope and imagines that it is a snake. Horror will overcome him, and he will shake from fear, anticipating in his mind all the agonies caused by the serpent's venomous bite. What a relief does this man experience when he sees that the rope is no snake. The cause of his fright lies in his error, his ignorance, his illusion. If the true nature of the rope is recognised, his tranquillity of mind will come back to him; he will feel relieved; he will be joyful and happy.

"This is the state of mind of one who has recognised that there is no self, that the cause of all his troubles, cares, and vanities is a mirage, a shadow, a dream.

"Happy is he who has overcome all selfishness; happy is he who has attained peace; happy is he who has found the truth.

"The truth is noble and sweet; the truth can deliver you from evil. There is no saviour in the world except the truth.

"Have confidence in the truth, although you may not be able to comprehend it, although you may suppose its sweetness to be bitter, although you may shrink from it at first. Trust in the truth.

"The truth is best as it is. No one can alter it; neither can any one improve it. Have faith in the truth and live it.

"Errors lead astray; illusions beget miseries. They intoxicate like strong drinks; but they fade away soon and leave you sick and disgusted. Self is a fever; self is a transient vision, a dream; but truth is wholesome, truth is sublime, truth is everlasting. There is no immortality except in truth. For truth alone abideth forever."

And when the doctrine was propounded, the venerable Kaundinya, the oldest one among the five *bhikshus*, discerned the truth with his mental eye, and he said: "Truly, O Buddha, our Lord, thou hast found the truth."

And the devas and saints and all the good spirits of the departed generations that had listened to the sermon of the Tathagata, joyfully received the doctrine and shouted: "Truly, the Blessed One has founded the kingdom of righteousness. The Blessed One has moved the earth; he has set the wheel of Truth rolling, which by no one in the universe, be he god or man, can ever be turned back. The kingdom of Truth will be preached upon earth; it will spread; and righteousness, good-will, and peace will reign among mankind."

✧ Bhagavad Gita ✧

The *Bhagavad Gita* ("The Lord's Song") is probably the best-known and best-loved document in all of Indian religious literature. As it has come down to us, it forms part of Book VI of the *Mahabharata*. The *Mahabharata* probably originated in oral accounts of a great battle fought in about the ninth century BCE. Part heroic tale, part religious lesson, it tells the story of the battle fought on the plains near modern Delhi between the sons of the blind king Dhritarastra and their cousins, the rightful heirs to the throne.

Because of his blindness, Dhritarastra yielded his throne to his younger brother Pandu. Pandu had five sons, all secretly fathered by deities, who were known as Pandavas from their father's name. Dhritarastra, who had a hundred sons, divided his kingdom between his sons and Pandu's sons. The five Pandava brothers were raised at Dhritarastra's court. They excelled in every competition, incurring the jealousy of Dhritarastra's heir Duryodana. Duryodana cheated his cousin, the Pandava king Yudhishtra, out of his kingdom and then reneged on a promise to restore it to him after Yudhishra spent twelve years in exile. The god Krishna attempted to prevent war, but when it seemed inevitable, he decided to serve the outnumbered Pandavas as the charioteer of Yudhishtra's brother, the great archer Arjuna. In the eighteen-day war that followed, most of the combatants perished.

Over the centuries bards and poets added to the *Mahabharata,* until it now consists of some 100,000 couplets and is the world's longest poem. As the product of many centuries of development, it exhibits a wide variety of attitudes. About four-fifths of the whole are episodes having little connection with the main story. The *Mahabharata* was probably completed in its present form by the second century BCE, though some revisions were undoubtedly made later.

In eighteen brief chapters or "teachings," the *Gita* centers on the concept of *yoga*, or "spiritual discipline." There are many kinds of *yoga* in India and elsewhere today, but the *Gita* emphasizes three: *karma yoga, jnana yoga*, and *bhakti yoga*. The word *karma* (often mistranslated as "fate") is from a root meaning "to do" and is translated as "action." *Karma yoga* is the "discipline of action"; it means to adhere to one's duty (*dharma*) while remaining detached from the reward. *Jnana* in Sanskrit means "knowledge" or "discernment" and is cognate with the Greek word *gnosis*, which has acquired a similar meaning of "spiritual knowledge" in English. *Jnana yoga*, the "discipline of knowledge," is a means of seeking salvation by developing identification with the real self (*atman*, also translated as "soul") rather than with the body or ego. The root of *bhakti* means "to be attached to God." Later in the *Gita*, Krishna says that devotion to God (*bhakti yoga*) is the supreme *yoga*. This concept became more widespread later in Indian history than the previous two.

The *Gita* takes place just before the great battle on the plain of Kurukshetra ("field of the Kurus"). Arjuna foresees that this battle will prove disastrous for both sides. But Arjuna is also a *Kshatriya*—a member of the hereditary warrior class—and as such is duty-bound to fight bravely. He is forced to resolve the conflict between two apparently conflicting *dharmas*—the duty of family members to respect their relatives and teachers, and the no less stringent duty of the warrior to fight.

The entire *Gita* is cast in the form of a report by the charioteer Sanjaya to Dhritarastra. Some scholars prefer to regard it as the creation of a unique, inspired poet. But it is difficult to believe that a single author would include the contradictions, unnecessary repetitions, and irrelevant dialogue. It is more likely that diverse religious statements were gradually added to an original *Gita* narrative that focused on the impending battle.

The following extracts are taken from the first three lessons, in which Krishna presents two conflicting explanations why Arjuna needs to fight. One emphasizes *karma yoga* as the path to salvation. Individuals must fulfill their obligations, but must do so without selfish attachment to personal satisfactions. The other explanation mentions *jnana yoga*. In the middle six lessons, the focus shifts toward knowledge of Krishna and presents the idea of *bhakti yoga* as the highest path to salvation. The final six lessons explore various ways of reconciling the apparent contradictions of the previous lessons.

A vast number of images from the *Bhagavad Gita* can be found on the Internet. Some of the most extensive are at http://www.bhagavad-gita.us.

Questions

1. According to the *Bhagavad Gita*, how should we conduct ourselves in our daily lives? How can we obtain the highest good?
2. What questions does Arjuna ask Krishna regarding life and death? How does Krishna answer these questions? What impact does such knowledge have on everyday actions?
3. What is the *Bhagavad Gita*'s attitude toward war?
4. Compare the advice of Krishna to Arjuna with that of the Buddha regarding *dharma*, which the *Bhagavad Gita* interprets as divinely ordained duty. How does the Buddha define the term in the two texts?
5. The *Bhagavad Gita* is said to have a universality that crosses time and place. What relevance does its message possess for you?

Bhagavad Gita

Edwin Arnold, trans., *The Song Celestial; or Bhagavad-gītā (from the Mahābhārata) Being a Discourse between Arjuna, Prince of India, and the Supreme Being under the Form of Krishna* (Boston: Roberts Brothers, 1885)

The First Teaching

Arjuna's Dejection

Arjuna, his war flag a rampant monkey, saw Dhritarashtra's sons assembled as weapons were ready to clash, and he lifted his bow.

He told his charioteer:
"Krishna, halt my chariot between the armies!
Far enough for me to see these men who lust for
war, ready to fight with me in the strain of battle.
I see men gathered here, eager to fight,
bent on serving the folly of Dhritarashtra's son."[1]
When Arjuna had spoken, Krishna halted
their splendid chariot between the armies.
Facing Bhishma[2] and Drona[3] and all the great kings,
he said, "Arjuna, see the Kuru men assembled here!"
Arjuna saw them standing there: fathers, grandfathers,
teachers, uncles, brothers, sons, grandsons, and friends.
He surveyed his elders and companions in both armies,
all his kinsmen assembled together.
Dejected, filed with strange pity, he said this:
"Krishna, I see my kinsmen gathered here, wanting war.
My limbs sink, my mouth is parched, my body trembles,
the hair bristles on my flesh.
The magic bow slips from my hand, my skin burns,
I cannot stand still, my mind reels.
I see omens of chaos, Krishna; I see no
good in killing my kinsmen in battle.
Krishna, I seek no victory, or kingship or pleasures.
What use to us are kingship, delights, or life itself?
We sought kingship, delights, and pleasures for the sake of those
assembled to abandon their lives and fortunes in battle.
They are teachers, fathers, sons, and grandfathers, uncles, grandsons,
fathers and brothers of wives, and other men of our family.
I do not want to kill them even if I am killed, Krishna;
not for kingship of all three worlds, much less for the earth!
What joy is there for us, Krishna, in killing Dhritarashtra's sons?
Evil will haunt us if we kill them, though their bows are drawn
to kill.
Honor forbids us to kill our cousins, Dhritarashtra's sons;
how can we know happiness if we kill our own kinsmen?

[1] Duryodhana.
[2] Commander-in-chief of the Kurus.
[3] Revered teacher of both sides at Dhritarashtra's court.

The greed that distorts their reason blinds them to the sin they commit
in ruining the family, blinds them to the crime of betraying friends.
How can we ignore the wisdom of turning from this evil
when we see the sin of family destruction, Krishna?
When the family is ruined, the timeless laws of family duty perish;
and when duty is lost, chaos overwhelms the family.
In overwhelming chaos, Krishna, women of the family are corrupted;[4]
and when women are corrupted, disorder is born in society.
This discord drags the violators and the family itself to hell
for ancestors fall when rites of offering rice and water lapse.
The sins of men who violate the family create disorder in society that
undermines the constant laws of caste and family duty.
Krishna, we have heard that a place in hell
is reserved for men who undermine family duties.
I lament the great sin we commit when our greed
for kingship and pleasures drives us to kill our kinsmen.
If Dhritarashtra's armed sons kill me in battle when I am
unarmed and offer no resistance, it will be my reward."
Saying this in the time of war, Arjuna slumped into the chariot
and laid down his bow and arrows, his mind tormented
by grief.

The Second Teaching

Philosophy and Spiritual Discipline

Sanjaya

Arjuna sat dejected, filed with pity, his sad eyes blurred by tears.
Krishna gave him counsel.

Lord Krishna

Why this cowardice in time of crisis, Arjuna?
The coward is ignoble, shameful, foreign to the ways of
heaven.

[4] Probably a reference to marriage outside their caste.

Don't yield to impotence! It is unnatural in you!
Banish this petty weakness from your heart.
Rise to the fight, Arjuna!

Arjuna

Krishna, how can I fight against Bhishma and Drona
with arrows when they deserve my worship?
It is better in this world to beg for scraps of food than to eat meals
smeared with the blood of elders I killed at the height of their power while their goals were still desires.
We don't know which weight is worse to bear—
our conquering them or their conquering us.
We will not want to live if we kill
the sons of Dhritarashtra assembled before us.
The flaw of pity blights my very being;
conflicting sacred duties confound my reason.
I ask you to tell me decisively—Which is better?
I am your pupil. Teach me what I seek!
I see nothing that could drive away
the grief that withers my senses;
even if I won kingdoms of unrivaled wealth
on earth and sovereignty over gods.

Sanjaya

Arjuna told this to Krishna—then saying, "I shall not fight," he fell silent.
Mocking him gently, Krishna gave this counsel as Arjuna sat dejected,
between the two armies.

Lord Krishna

You grieve for those beyond grief, and you speak words of insight;
but learned men do not grieve for the dead or the living.
Never have I not existed nor you, nor these kings;
and never in the future shall we cease to exist.
Just as the embodied self[5] enters childhood, youth, and old age,
so does it enter another body; this does not confound a steadfast man.

---

[5] *atman.*

Contacts with matter make us feel heat and cold, pleasure and pain.
Arjuna, you must learn to endure fleeting things—they come and go!
When these cannot torment a man, when suffering and joy are equal for him and he has courage, he is fit for immortality.
Nothing of nonbeing comes to be, nor does being cease to exist;
the boundary between these two is seen by men who see reality.
Indestructible is the presence that pervades all this;
no one can destroy this unchanging reality.
Our bodies are known to end, but the embodied self is enduring,
indestructible, and immeasurable; therefore, Arjuna, fight the battle!
He who thinks this self a killer and he who thinks it killed,
both fail to understand; it does not kill, nor is it killed.
It is not born, it does not die; having been, it will never not be;
unborn, enduring, constant, and primordial,
it is not killed when the body is killed.
Arjuna, when a man knows the self to be indestructible, enduring,
unborn, unchanging, how does he kill or cause anyone to kill?
As a man discards worn-out clothes to put on new and different ones,[6]
so the embodied self discards its worn-out bodies to take on other new ones.
Weapons do not cut it, fire does not burn it,
waters do not wet it, wind does not wither it.
It cannot be cut or burned; it cannot be wet or withered;
it is enduring, all-pervasive, fixed, immovable, and timeless.
It is called unmanifest, inconceivable, and immutable;
since you know that to be so, you should not grieve!
If you think of its birth and death as ever-recurring,
then too, Great Warrior, you have no cause to grieve!
Death is certain for anyone born, and birth is certain for the dead;
since the cycle is inevitable, you have no cause to grieve!

[6] This refers to *samsara*, the transmigration of the self to a new body when a person dies.

Creatures are unmanifest in origin, manifest in the midst of life,
and unmanifest again in the end.
Since this is so, why do you lament?
Rarely someone sees it, rarely another speaks it,
rarely anyone hears it—even hearing it, no one really knows it.
The self embodied in the body of every being is indestructible;
you have no cause to grieve for all these creatures, Arjuna!
Look to your own duty; do not tremble before it;
nothing is better for a warrior than a battle of sacred duty.
The doors of heaven open for warriors who rejoice
to have a battle like this thrust on them by chance.
If you fail to wage this war of sacred duty,
you will abandon your own duty and fame only to gain evil.
People will tell of your undying shame,
and for a man of honor shame is worse than death.
The great chariot warriors will think you deserted in fear of battle;
you will be despised by those who held you in esteem.
Your enemies will slander you, scorning your skill
in so many unspeakable ways—could any suffering be worse?
If you are killed, you win heaven; if you triumph, you enjoy the earth;
therefore, Arjuna, stand up and resolve to fight the battle!
Impartial to joy and suffering, gain and loss, victory and defeat,
arm yourself for the battle, lest you fall into evil.
Understanding is defined in terms of philosophy;
now hear it in spiritual discipline.
Armed with this understanding, Arjuna,
you will escape the bondage of action.
No effort in this world is lost or wasted;
a fragment of sacred duty saves you from great fear.
This understanding is unique in its inner core of resolve;
diffuse and pointless are the ways irresolute men understand.
Undiscerning men who delight in the tenets of ritual lore
utter florid speech, proclaiming, "There is nothing else!"
Driven by desire, they strive after heaven and contrive to win powers and delights, but their intricate ritual language bears only the fruit of action in rebirth.

Obsessed with powers and delights, their reason lost in words,
they do not find in contemplation this understanding of inner resolve.
Arjuna, the realm of sacred lore is nature—beyond its triad of qualities,
dualities, and mundane rewards, be forever lucid, alive to your self.
For the discerning priest, all of sacred lore
has no more value than a well when water flows everywhere.
Be intent on action, not on the fruits of action;
avoid attraction to the fruits and attachment to inaction!
Perform actions, firm in discipline, relinquishing attachment;
be impartial to failure and success—this equanimity is called discipline.
Arjuna, action is far inferior to the discipline of understanding;[7]
so seek refuge in understanding—pitiful are men drawn by fruits of action.
Disciplined by understanding, one abandons both good and evil deeds;
so arm yourself for discipline—discipline is skill in actions.
Wise men disciplined by understanding relinquish the fruit born of
action; freed from these bonds of rebirth, they reach a place beyond decay.
When your understanding passes beyond the swamp of delusion,
you will be indifferent to all that is heard in sacred lore.
When your understanding turns from sacred lore to stand fixed,
immovable in contemplation, then you will reach discipline.

Arjuna

Krishna, what defines a man deep in contemplation whose insight
and thought are sure? How would he speak?
How would he sit? How would he move?

Lord Krishna

When he gives up desires in his mind, is content with the self within
himself, then he is said to be a man whose insight is sure, Arjuna.
When suffering does not disturb his mind, when his craving for pleasures
has vanished, when attraction, fear, and anger are gone, he is called a sage whose thought is sure.

---

[7] *jnana yoga.*

When he shows no preference in fortune or misfortune
and neither exults nor hates, his insight is sure.
When, like a tortoise retracting its limbs, he withdraws his senses
completely from sensuous objects, his insight is sure.
Sensuous objects fade when the embodied self abstains from food;
the taste lingers, but it too fades in the vision of higher truth.
Even when a man of wisdom tries to control them, Arjuna,
the bewildering senses attack his mind with violence.
Controlling them all, with discipline he should focus on me;
when his senses are under control, his insight is sure.
Brooding about sensuous objects makes attachment to them grow;
from attachment desire arises, from desire anger is born.
From anger comes confusion; from confusion memory lapses;
from broken memory understanding is lost; from loss of understanding, he is ruined.
But a man of inner strength whose senses experience objects
without attraction and hatred, in self-control, finds serenity.
In serenity, all his sorrows dissolve;
his reason becomes serene, his understanding sure.
Without discipline, he has no understanding or inner power;
without inner power, he has no peace; and without peace where is joy?
If his mind submits to the play of the senses,
they drive away insight, as wind drives a ship on water.
So, Great Warrior, when withdrawal of the senses
from sense objects is complete, discernment[8] is firm.
When it is night for all creatures, a master of restraint is awake;
when they are awake, it is night for the sage who sees reality.
As the mountainous depths of the ocean are unmoved when waters rush into it, so the man unmoved when desires enter him attains a peace that eludes the man of many desires.
When he renounces all desires and acts without craving,
possessiveness, or individuality, he finds peace.
This is the place of the infinite spirit; achieving it, one is freed from delusion; abiding in it even at the time of death, one finds the pure calm of infinity.

---

[8] i.e., *jnana yoga*.

The Third Teaching

Discipline of Action

Arjuna
If you think understanding is more powerful than action,
why, Krishna, do you urge me to this horrific act?
You confuse my understanding with a maze of words;
speak one certain truth so I may achieve what is good.

Lord Krishna
Earlier I taught the twofold basis of good in this world
for philosophers, disciplined knowledge; for men of discipline, action.
A man cannot escape the force of action by abstaining from actions;
he does not attain success just by renunciation.
No one exists for even an instant without performing action;
however unwilling, every being is forced to act by the qualities of nature.
When his senses are controlled but he keeps recalling
sense objects with his mind, he is a self-deluded hypocrite.
When he controls his senses with his mind and engages in the discipline of action with his faculties of action, detachment sets him apart.
Perform necessary action; it is more powerful than inaction;
without action you even fail to sustain your own body.
Action imprisons the world unless it is done as sacrifice;
freed from attachment, Arjuna, perform action as sacrifice!
When creating living beings and sacrifice, Prajapati, the primordial creator, said:

"By sacrifice will you procreate!
Let it be your wish-granting cow!
Foster the gods with this,
and may they foster you;
by enriching one another,
you will achieve a higher good.
Enriched by sacrifice, the gods
will give you the delights you desire;
he is a thief who enjoys their gifts
without giving to them in return."

Good men eating the remnants of sacrifice are free of any guilt,
but evil men who cook for themselves eat the food of sin.
Creatures depend on food, food comes from rain,
rain depends on sacrifice, and sacrifice comes from action.
Action comes from the spirit of prayer, whose source is OM, sound of the imperishable; so the pervading infinite spirit is ever present in rites of sacrifice.
He who fails to keep turning the wheel here set in motion
wastes his life in sin, addicted to the senses, Arjuna.
But when a man finds delight within himself and feels inner joy
and pure contentment in himself, there is nothing more to be done.
He has no stake here in deeds done or undone,
nor does his purpose depend on other creatures.
Always perform with detachment any action you must do;
performing action with detachment, one achieves supreme good.
Janaka[9] and other ancient kings attained perfection by action alone;
seeing the way to preserve the world, you should act.
Whatever a leader does, the ordinary people also do.
He sets the standard for the world to follow.
In the three worlds, there is nothing I must do,
nothing unattained to be attained, yet I engage in action.
What if I did not engage relentlessly in action?
Men retrace my path at every turn, Arjuna.
These worlds would collapse if I did not perform action;
I would create disorder in society, living beings would be destroyed.
As the ignorant act with attachment to actions, Arjuna,
so wise men should act with detachment to preserve the world.
No wise man disturbs the understanding of ignorant men attached to action;
he should inspire them, performing all actions with discipline.
Actions are all effected by the qualities of nature;
but deluded by individuality, the self thinks, "I am the actor."

---

[9] King of Mithila who sacrificed to the gods personally, rather than through a Brahman priest, and thus became a Brahman through his own efforts. Janaka was also the father-in-law of Rama, hero of the epic *Ramayana*.

When he can discriminate the actions of nature's qualities and think,
"The qualities depend upon other qualities," he is detached.
Those deluded by the qualities of nature are attached to their actions;
a man who knows this should not upset these dull men of partial knowledge.
Surrender all actions to me, and fix your reason on your inner self;
without hope or possessiveness, your fever subdued, fight the battle!
Men who always follow my thought, trusting it without finding fault,
are freed even by their actions.
But those who find fault and fail to follow my thought, know that
they are lost fools, deluded by every bit of knowledge.
Even a man of knowledge behaves in accord with his own nature;
creatures all conform to nature; what can one do to restrain them?
Attraction and hatred are poised in the object of every sense experience;
a man must not fall prey to these two brigands lurking on his path!
Your own duty done imperfectly is better than another man's done well.
It is better to die in one's own duty; another man's duty is perilous.

Arjuna
Krishna, what makes a person commit evil
against his own will, as if compelled by force?

Lord Krishna
It is desire and anger, arising from nature's quality of passion;
know it here as the enemy, voracious and very evil!
As fire is obscured by smoke and a mirror by dirt,
as an embryo is veiled by its caul, so is knowledge obscured by this.
Knowledge is obscured by the wise man's eternal enemy,
which takes form as desire, an insatiable fire, Arjuna.
The senses, mind, and understanding are said to harbor desire;
with these desire obscures knowledge and confounds the embodied self.

Therefore, first restrain your senses, Arjuna;
then kill this evil that ruins knowledge and judgment.
Men say that the senses are superior to their objects, the mind superior to the senses, understanding superior to the mind; higher than understanding is the self.
Knowing the self beyond understanding, sustain the self with the self.
Great Warrior, kill the enemy menacing you in the form of desire!

✧ Arthasastra ✧

Kautilya

Throughout most of its history, India was composed of numerous weak, fragmented, and decentralized states that displayed little stability. Although some states persisted for generations as the territorial base of power of a single family, more commonly boundaries and ruling families changed constantly. Petty courts throughout India replicated those of the richer and more powerful states, but on a smaller scale. Rulers patronized the Brahmans, or priestly caste, employing them to perform state rituals and allowing them great authority as administrators and advisers. The religious recognition accorded by the Brahmans gave the kings greater legitimacy, but also the influence of the Brahmans limited the ability of the kings to act independently.

During exceptional periods of unity great empires arose, such as when Chandragupta Maurya (r. 320–298 BCE) united all but the southernmost tip of India. This Mauryan Empire did not last, however, and fragmented a generation after the death of Asoka, popularly known as Asoka the Great and one of India's greatest emperors, in 232 BCE. The later Gupta Empire (c. 320–500 CE) achieved cultural grandeur, but its political power was restricted to northern India.

The *Arthasastra*, a treatise on statecraft, economic policy, and military strategy, is attributed to Kautilya, a legendary figure based probably on a historic person, whose personal name was Chanakya. Tradition states that Kautilya was a minister to Chandragupta Maurya. Although the *Arthasastra* as it stands today was written by several hands and compiled from earlier texts into its present form sometime between 150 and 250 CE, it reflects the Machiavellian politics of the Mauryan era. Its fifteen books cover all aspects of governing, divided into 180 topics. While the *Bhagavad Gita* is concerned with two of the four ends of life, *dharma*, or religiously ordained duty, and *moksha*, salvation, the *Arthasastra* concerns itself with *artha*, or material gain (the fourth is *kama*, or physical pleasure).

The *Arthasastra* describes a political system of many small states, each either the ally or the enemy of the others. Warfare was endemic, but had little effect on the basic cultural and economic life of the region. The goal of battle was "righteous victory" (*dharmavijaya*), in which the conqueror released his enemy unharmed, without looting or destroying the capital, and the conquered admitted his subservience, at least for a time. These many weak kingdoms prevented one strong kingdom from arising. Although each of the petty kings surrounded himself with an aura of divinity, this emphasis on appearances brought no real stability to the system. Political alignments were in a constant state of flux, boundaries changed constantly, and kings fell, only to be replaced by others. Ruling dynasties disappeared from historical records, only to reappear centuries later. This fluid and segmented political system nevertheless coexisted within a stable and confident civilization, tolerant of cultural diversity but resistant to change.

The warfare of the kings had little lasting effect at the local level, where society was regulated by caste and custom, and ruled by prominent families of the district, who were often Brahmans. Indian life was concentrated in its thousands of agricultural villages, where the pace of life was dictated by the seasons and it seemed as if very little ever changed. The peasant would still pay taxes, often to the same tax collector, regardless of which king ended up with the revenue. Without the homogenizing effect of a strong central ruler, local customs persisted and village life remained relatively unaltered by time. This stability at the local level promoted extraordinary conservatism. Indian civilization maintained continuity throughout this era, but it was the continuity of a religious and cultural tradition based on popular participation, rather than of political institutions imposed from above.

The *Arthasastra* continued to be influential until the twelfth century, when it disappeared. In 1905, Rudrapatnam Shamasastry, chief librarian of the Mysore Government Oriental Library, rediscovered the text of the *Arthasastra*. Shamasastry published several editions of the text and translated it into English.

To read an interesting article on Shamasastry's discovery of the *Arthasastra*, go to http://www.vakmumbai.org.

Questions

1. What is the role of Brahmans in the political system?
2. How does a ruler determine whether another ruler is a friend or a foe?
3. What are the conditions necessary for peace?
4. How would a Daoist respond to the assertion in the *Arthasastra* that the root of well-being is found in activity?

Arthasastra

Rudrapatnam Shamasastry, trans., *Kautilya's Arthaśāstra* (Bangalore: Government Press, 1915), pp. 36–39, 287, 289–296

Section 16 Rules for the King

1 When the king is active, the servants become active following his example. 2 If he is remiss, they too become remiss along with him. 3 And they consume his works. 4 Moreover, he is over-reached by enemies. 5 Therefore, he should himself be (energetically) active.

6 He should divide the day into eight parts as also the night by means of *nalikas*, or by the measure of the shadow (of the gnomon).

7 (A shadow) measuring three *paurusas*, one *paurusa*, (and) four *angulas*, and the midday when the shadow disappears, these are the four earlier eighth parts of the day. 8 By them are explained the later (four). 9 Out of them, during the first eighth part of the day, he should listen to measures taken for defence and (accounts of) income and expenditure. 10 During the second, he should look into the affairs of the citizens and the country people. 11 During the third, he should take his bath and meals and devote himself to study. 12 During the fourth, he should receive revenue in cash and assign tasks to heads of departments. 13 During the fifth, he should consult the council of ministers by sending letters, and acquaint himself with secret information brought in by spies. 14 During the sixth, he should engage in recreation at his pleasure or hold consultations. 15 During the seventh, he should review elephants, horses, chariots, and troops. 16 During the eighth, he should deliberate on military plans with the commander-in-chief. 17 When the day is ended, he should worship the evening twilight.

18 During the first (eighth) part of the night, he should interview secret agents. 19 During the second, he should take a bath and meals and engage in study. 20 During the third, he should go to bed to the strains of musical instruments and sleep during the fourth and the fifth (parts). 21 During the sixth, he should awaken to the sound of musical instruments and ponder over the teaching of the science (of politics) as well as over the work to be done. 22 During the seventh, he should sit in consultation (with councillors) and despatch secret agents. 23 During the eighth, he should receive blessings from priests, preceptors and chaplain, and see his physician, chief cook and astrologer. 24 And after going round a cow with her calf and a bull, he should proceed to the assembly hall.

25 Or, he should divide the day and night into (different) parts in conformity with his capacity and carry out his tasks.

26 Arriving in the assembly hall, he should allow unrestricted entrance to those wishing to see him in connection with their affairs. 27 For, a king difficult of access is made to do the reverse of what ought to be done and what ought not to be done, by those near him. 28 In consequence of that, he may have to face an insurrection of the subjects or subjugation by the enemy. 29 Therefore, he should look into the affairs of temple deities, hermitages, heretics, Brahmans learned in the Vedas, cattle and holy places, of minors, the aged, the sick, the distressed and the helpless and of women, in (this) order, or, in accordance with the importance of the matter or its urgency.

30 He should hear (at once) every urgent matter, (and) not put it off. An (affair) postponed becomes difficult to settle or even impossible to settle. 31 He should look into the affairs of persons learned in the Vedas and of ascetics after going to the fire sanctuary (and) in the company of his chaplain and preceptor, after getting up from his seat and saluting (those suitors). 32 But he should decide the affairs of ascetics and of persons versed in the practice of magic, (in consultation) with persons learned in the three Vedas, not by himself (alone), for the reason that they might be roused to anger. 33 For the king, the (sacrificial) vow is activity, sacrifice the administration of affairs; the sacrificial fee, however, is impartiality of behaviour, (and) sacrificial initiation for him is the coronation.

34 In the happiness of the subjects lies the happiness of the king and in what is beneficial to the subjects his own benefit. What is dear to himself is not beneficial to the king, but what is dear to the subjects is beneficial (to him). 35 Therefore, being ever active, the king should carry out the

management of material well-being. The root of material well-being is activity, of material disaster its reverse.

36 In the absence of activity, there is certain destruction of what is obtained and of what is not yet received. By activity reward is obtained, and one also secures abundance of riches.

Section 96 Excellence of the Constituent Elements

1 The king, the minister, the country, the fortified city, the treasury, the army and the ally are the constituent elements (of the state).

2 Among them, the excellences of the king are:

3 Born in a high family, endowed with good fortune, intelligence and spirit, given to seeing elders, pious, truthful in speech, not breaking his promise, grateful, liberal, of great energy, not dilatory, with weak neighbouring princes, resolute, not having a mean council (of ministers), desirous of training—these are the qualities of one easily approachable.

4 Desire to learn, listening, learning, retention, thorough understanding, reflecting, rejecting (false views) and intentness on truth—these are the qualities of intellect.

5 Bravery, resentment, quickness, and dexterity—these are the qualities of energy.

6 Eloquent, bold, endowed with memory, intellect, and strength, exalted, easy to manage, trained in arts, free from vices, able to lead the army, able to requite obligations and injury in the prescribed manner, possessed of a sense of shame, able to take suitable action in calamities and in normal conditions, seeing long and far, attaching prominence to undertakings at the proper place and time and with appropriate human endeavour, able to discriminate between peace and fighting, giving and withholding, and (observance of) conditions and (striking at) the enemy's weak points, well-guarded, not laughing in an undignified manner, with a glance which is straight and without a frown, devoid of passion, anger, greed, stiffness, fickleness, troublesomeness, and slanderousness, sweet in speech, speaking with a smile and with dignity, with conduct conforming to the advice of elders,—these are personal excellences.

Section 97 Concerning Peace and Activity

1 Peace and activity constitute the source of acquisition and security.
2 Activity is that which brings about the accomplishment of works un-

dertaken. 3 Peace is that which brings about security of enjoyment of the fruits of works.

4 The source of peace and activity is the six-fold policy. 5 Decline, stability, and advancement are the consequences of that (policy).

6 (Acts) of human agency are good policy and bad policy; of divine agency good fortune and misfortune. 7 For, it is acts of human and divine agency that make the world go. 8 That caused by an unseen agency is the divine (act). 9 In that, the attainment of the desired fruit is good fortune; of undesired (fruit), misfortune. 10 That caused by a seen agency is the human (act). 11 In that, the coming into being of well-being is good policy; (its) ruin, bad policy. 12 That can be thought about; the divine is incalculable.

13 The king, endowed with personal excellences and those of his material constituents, the seat of good policy, is the would-be conqueror. 14 Encircling him on all sides, with territory immediately next to his is the constituent called the enemy. 15 In the same manner, one, with territory separated by one (other territory) is the constituent called the ally.

16 A neighbouring prince possessed of the excellences of an enemy is the foe; one in calamity is vulnerable; one without support or with a weak support is fit to be exterminated; in the reverse case, fit to be harassed or weakened. 17 These are the different types of enemies.

18 Beyond him, the ally, the enemy's ally, the ally's ally, and the enemy's ally's ally are situated in front in accordance with the proximity of the territories; behind, the enemy in the rear, the ally in the rear, the rear enemy's ally and the rear ally's ally (one behind the other).

19 One with immediately proximate territory is the natural enemy; one of equal birth is the enemy by birth; one opposed or in opposition is the enemy made (for the time being).

20 One with territory separated by one other is the natural ally; one related through the mother or father is the ally by birth; one who has sought shelter for wealth or life is the ally made (for the time being).

21 One with territory immediately proximate to those of the enemy and the conqueror, capable of helping them when they are united or disunited and of suppressing them when they are disunited, is the middle king.

22 One outside (the sphere of) the enemy, the conqueror and the middle king, stronger than (their) constituents, capable of helping the enemy, the conqueror and the middle king when they are united or disunited and of suppressing them when they are disunited, is the neutral king.

23 These are the constituents (of the circle of kings).

24 Or, the conqueror, the ally and the ally's ally are the three constituents of this (circle of kings). 25 They, each individually united with its five constituent elements, the minister, the country, the fort, the treasury, and the army, constitute the eighteen-fold circle. 26 By that is explained a separate circle (for each of) the enemy, the middle, and the neutral kings. 27 Thus there is a collection of four circles.

28 There are twelve constituents who are kings, sixty material constituents, a total of seventy-two in all. 29 Each of these has its own peculiar excellences.

30 Power and success (are to be explained). 31 Power is (possession of) strength. 32 Success is (obtaining) happiness.

33 Power is three-fold: the power of knowledge is the power of counsel, the power of the treasury and the army is the power of might, the power of valour is the power of energy.

34 In the same way, success is also three-fold: that attainable by the power of counsel is success by counsel, that attainable by the power of might is success by might, that attainable by the power of energy is success by energy.

35 Thriving with these, the (king) becomes superior; reduced (in these), inferior; with equal powers, equal. 36 Therefore, he should endeavour to endow himself with power and success, or, if similar, (to endow with power and success) the material constituents in accordance with their immediate proximity or integrity. 37 Or, he should endeavour to detract (these) from treasonable persons and enemies.

38 Or, if he were to see [that], "My enemy, possessed of power, will injure his subjects with verbal or physical injury or appropriation of their property, or, when endowed with success, will become negligent because of (addiction to) hunting, gambling, wine or women, thus with subjects disaffected or (himself) become weakened or remiss, he will be easy to overpower for me; or, being attacked in war, he will remain in one place or not in his fort, with all his troops collected together, thus with his army brought together, (and himself) separated from his ally and fort, he will be easy to overpower for me; or, he will render help to me when I am attacked by a strong king, (thinking) 'the strong king is desirous of exterminating my enemy elsewhere; after exterminating him, he might exterminate me,' or (help me) when my undertakings have failed"; and when seeking to seize the middle king (the enemy's help is needed);—for these and other reasons, he may wish power and success even to the enemy.

39 Making the kings separated by one (intervening territory) the ally and those immediately proximate the spokes, the leader should stretch himself out as the hub in the circle of constituents.

40 For, the enemy situated between the two, the leader and the ally, becomes easy to exterminate or to harass, even if strong.

Herewith ends the Sixth Book of the Arthasastra of Kautilya "The Circle (of Kings) as the Basis."

Section 99 Determination of (Measures in) Decline, Stable Condition, and Advancement

1 The circle of constituent elements is the basis of the six measures of foreign policy.

2 "Peace, war, staying quiet, marching, seeking shelter, and dual policy constitute the six measures," say the teachers.

3 "There are (only) two measures," says Vatavyadhi. 4 "For, out of peace and war the six measures come into being." 5 "These are really six measures, because of differences in the situations," says Kautilya.

6 Among them, entering into a treaty is peace. 7 Doing injury is war. 8 Remaining indifferent is staying quiet. 9 Augmentation of (powers) is marching. 10 Submitting to another is seeking shelter. 11 Resorting to peace (with one) and war (with another) is dual policy. 12 These are the six measures of foreign policy.

13 When in decline as compared to the enemy, he should make peace. 14 When prospering, he should make war. 15 (When he thinks) "The enemy is not able to do harm to me, nor I to him," he should stay quiet. 16 When possessed of a preponderance of excellent qualities, he should march. 17 Depleted in power, he should seek shelter. 18 In a work that can be achieved with the help of an associate, he should resort to a dual policy. 19 Thus are the measures established.

20 Of them, he should follow that policy by resorting to which he may be able to see [that], "By resorting to this, I shall be able to promote my own undertakings concerning forts, water-works, trade-routes, settling on waste land, mines, material forests and elephant forests, and to injure these undertakings of the enemy." 21 That is advancement. 22 Perceiving "My advancement will be quicker or greater or leading to a greater advancement in the future, the reverse (will be) that of the enemy," he should remain indifferent to the enemy's advancement. 23 In case the

advancement takes the same time or bears an equal fruit (for both), he should make peace.

24 He should not follow that policy by resorting to which he were to see the ruin of his own undertakings, not of (those of) the other (party). 25 This is decline. 26 Perceiving "I shall decline after a longer time or to a lesser extent or in such a way that I shall make a greater advancement, the enemy (will decline) in the reverse manner," he should remain indifferent to his decline. 27 In case the decline lasts for the same period or leads to equal results (for both), he should make peace.

28 The policy, following which he were to see neither the advancement nor the decline of his own undertakings, constitutes stable condition. 29 Perceiving "I shall remain stable for a shorter period or in such a way that I shall make a greater advancement, the enemy (will do so) in the opposite way," he should remain indifferent to his stable condition. 30 "In case the stable condition lasts for the same period or leads to equal consequences (for both), he should make peace," say the teachers. 31 This is not disputed, says Kautilya.

32 Or, if he were to see [that], "Remaining at peace, I shall ruin the enemy's undertakings by my own undertakings bearing abundant fruits; or, I shall enjoy my own undertakings bearing abundant fruits or the undertakings of the enemy; or, by creating confidence by means of the peace, I shall ruin the enemy's undertakings by the employment of secret remedies and occult practices; or, I shall easily entice away the persons capable of carrying out the enemy's undertakings by (offering) a greater remuneration from my own undertakings, with facilities of favours and exemptions; or, the enemy, in alliance with an extremely strong king, will suffer the ruin of his own undertakings; or, I shall keep prolonged his war with the king, being at war with whom he is making peace with me; or, he will harass the country of the king, who is in alliance with me (but is) hostile to me; or, his country, laid waste by his enemy, will come to me, so that I shall achieve advancement in my undertakings; or, the enemy, with his undertakings ruined (and himself) placed in a difficult situation, would not attack my undertakings; or, with my undertakings started elsewhere, I shall achieve advancement in my undertakings, being in alliance with both; or, by making peace with the enemy I shall divide from him the circle of (kings) which is attached to the enemy, (and) when divided, I shall secure it (for myself); or, by giving support to the enemy by favouring him with troops when he seeks to seize the circle, I shall create hostility towards him, (and) when he faces hostility I shall

get him destroyed by that same (circle)," he should secure advancement through peace.

33 Or, if he were to see [that], "My country, consisting mostly of martial people or fighting bands, or secure in the protection of a single entrance through a mountain-fort, a forest-fort or a river-fort, will be able to repulse the enemy's attack; or, taking shelter in an impregnable fort on the border of my territory, I shall be able to ruin the enemy's undertakings; or, the enemy, with his energy sapped by the troubles caused by a calamity, has reached a time when his undertakings face ruin; or, when he is fighting elsewhere, I shall be able to carry off his country," he should secure advancement by resorting to war.

34 Or, if he were to think, "The enemy is not able to ruin my undertakings nor am I able to ruin his undertakings; or, (when) he is in a calamity, or (engaged) as in a conflict between a hound and a boar, I shall advance (myself), being intent on carrying out my own undertakings," he should secure advancement by staying quiet.

35 Or, if he were to think, "The ruin of the enemy's undertakings can be brought about by marching, and I have taken steps to secure the protection of my own undertakings," he should secure advancement by marching. 36 Or, if he were to think, "I am not able to ruin the enemy's undertakings nor to avert the ruin of my own undertakings," he should seek shelter with a strong king and by carrying out his own undertakings, should seek to progress from decline to stable condition and from stable condition to advancement. 37 Or, if he were to think, "I shall promote my own undertakings by peace on one side and ruin the enemy's undertakings by war on the other side," he should secure advancement through a dual policy.

38 Situated in the circle of constituent elements, he should, in this manner, with these six measures of policy, seek to progress from decline to stable condition and from stable condition to advancement in his own udertakings.

✧ Poems of Love and War ✧

Although cultural influences spread throughout the Indian subcontinent, south India remained politically independent of the north until the British conquest. South Indians spoke languages of an entirely different family, Dravidian, than north India. The oldest of these languages, Tamil, was regularized about 250 BCE and is less influenced by Sanskrit than any other Indian language. It produced a classical literature during the period from 150 BCE to 250 CE, of which several anthologies of poems survive. There are about 150 million speakers of Dravidian languages today.

Indian civilization took a different form in the Dravidian kingdoms. The Indus Valley civilization may have spoken a Dravidian language and thus may have influenced Vedic society as well as south India. The Indus Valley script has never been deciphered, however, and the extent to which Dravidian culture originated in the Indus Valley is uncertain. In any case, agriculture did not appear in south India until centuries after the end of the Indus Valley civilization, and records of the Tamils date from hundreds of years later still.

There are no reliable historical records from the period in which the poems were composed, but the surviving texts tell us much about the society. The poems are primarily secular and deal with love, war, governance, trade, and mourning. South India was divided into three kingdoms, the Pandyas, the Cōlas, and the Cheras. The region had no major external threats. Classical Tamil poetry is called "Sangam" poetry because it was later anthologized by a literary academy that called itself *sangam* (from the name for a Buddhist community of monks, or *sangha*). The academy claimed that two ancient *sangams* that preceded it had produced the poems. There is no historical evidence for the existence of these earlier academies, and the poems themselves clearly were composed by many different authors at different times and places. The fact that the poems were compiled at a later date suggests that more literature may not have found its way into the compilations and is lost.

Tamil poetics are described in the treatise *Tolkappiyam*, written in about the year 300. Early Tamil poetry is predominantly secular and is divided into two categories, *akam* (interior, or subjective, pronounced "aham") and *puram* (exterior, or objective). Love poems fall into the first category, war into the second. The primary elements of Tamil poetics are location (landscapes) and time (both the seasons of the year and the six parts of the day). The five landscapes of *akam* poetry are hills, forests, farmland, seashore, and wasteland. *Akam* poems are also shaped by "native elements," or relations between humans and nature, and "human elements," usually the stages of a love affair. *Puram* poetry has seven landscapes, corresponding to the phases of combat: cattle raiding, invasion, siege, pitched battle, victory, death, and praise of kings. (The latter two were not considered suitable for poetry.) Within this framework the Sangam poets created a moving literature.

In the first poem, for example, the *kuriñci* and the mountain scene clearly mark this as a poem about lovers meeting. Their union is not described but only alluded to by the scene of the bees making honey from the flowers of the *kuriñci* plant (which comes to flower only after twelve years). The poem zooms from cosmic abstractions about the speaker's love to the mountain slopes, the bees, and the flower itself, suggesting her progression from idealized feeling to physical intimacy. All this is accomplished in a few lines. The remainder of the *akam* poems are also about lovers meeting, except for the last, which is from the genre *pālai* (wasteland), which describes the lovers' journey through wilderness.

The *puram* poems here describe warfare and its consequences. The last of the *puram* poems, "King Killi in Combat," is based on a historical incident that would have been well known to those who heard the poem. The Cōla king Killi wagered his kingdom on a wrestling match with a rival. The first part of the poem describes the frantic moves of a cobbler who must finish a cot for his wife, who by custom must deliver their baby on it. The situations are parallel: the movements of both are skillful. If the cobbler succeeds, the child will be born on the cot and they will rejoice; if King Killi succeeds, the kingdom will be reborn and the people will rejoice. The laburnam is not a symbol of a mood as it would be in an *akam* poem, but simply the emblem of a clan.

The final poem is exceptional, since most of the poems have few religious references. It a late classical poem of praise to Tirumāl, a god of the forests who was later identified with Vishnu. In this poem the classical form is adapted to the new devotional (*bhakti*) Hinduism.

The translator of these poems, A.K. Ramanujan (1929–1993), was one of India's greatest modern poets as well as a noted scholar of Dravidian languages. These pieces are not only accurate translations of the letter and spirit of the originals, but works of elegant poetry in their own right. In these and other collections, Ramanujan brought to life one of the world's great literatures.

The absence of early historical records for south India has led to much fanciful speculation about the prehistory of Tamil speakers. The site http://archaeologyindia.com, incomplete at the time of this writing, attempts to illustrate as much of the early evidence as possible.

Questions

1. What to you are the most striking similarities and differences between the *akam* and *puram* poems?
2. Do the very stylized references to location, season, and time of day detract from the message of an *akam* poem or enhance it? Are there similarities in other love poems you have read?
3. The images of warfare in the *puram* poems are radically different from those in the *Bhagavad Gita.* Are there unifying themes in the two genres?

Poems of Love and War

A.K. Ramanujan, sel. and trans.,
Poems of Love and War from the Eight Anthologies and the Ten Long Poems of Classical Tamil
(New York: Columbia University Press, 1985),
pp. 5, 16, 17, 22–23, 63, 115–117, 120, 123, 179, 218

Akam Poems

What She Said

Bigger than earth, certainly,
higher than the sky,
more unfathomable than the waters
is this love for this man
of the mountain slopes
where bees make rich honey
from the flowers of the *kuriñci*
that has such black stalks.

Tēvakulattār
Kuruntokai 3

What He Said

As a little white snake
with lovely stripes on its young body
troubles the jungle elephant
this slip of a girl
her teeth like sprouts of new rice
her wrists stacked with bangles
troubles me.

Catti Nātanār
Kuruntokai 119

What She Said

Only the thief was there, no one else.
And if he should lie, what can I do?
There was only
a thin-legged heron standing
on legs yellow as millet stems
and looking
for lampreys
in the running water
when he took me

Kapilar
Kuruntokai 25

What Her Girl Friend Said to her

Their throats glittering like blue sapphire,
tail feathers splendid,
the peacocks gather
with sweet calls,
dancers skilled in slow-beat rhythms.
But you don't play anymore
like those peacocks
with your girl friends
in the long deep streams,
wearing wreaths of blue lily
with petals like eyes,
tresses flaring
as they dance.
Your heart is anxious,
you're lonely, stricken
with pallor.
Now, what shall I say to Mother
if she should notice changes
and ask for reasons?
I know,
our man from the mountain top
where long silver waterfalls shiver
in the wind
like white banners
borne high on elephants
with trappings on their brow,
I know
he has brought you these pangs.
But what shall I say to Mother
if she asks?

Maturai Marutanilanāicanār
Akanānūru 358

What He Said

The heart, knowing
no fear,

has left me
to go and hold my love
but my arms,
left behind,
cannot take hold.
So what's the use?
In the space between us,
murderous tigers
roar like dark ocean waves,
circling
in O how many woods
between us
and our arms' embrace

Allūr Nanmullai
Kuruntokai 237

Puram Poems

Harvest of War

Great king,
you shield your men from ruin,
so your victories, your greatness
are bywords.
Loose chariot wheels
lie about the battleground
with the long white tusks of
bull-elephants.
Flocks of male eagles
eat carrion
with their mates.
Headless bodies
dance about
before they fall
to the ground.
Blood glows,
like the sky before nightfall,
in the red center
of the battlefield.
Demons dance there.
And your kingdom

is an unfailing harvest
of victorious wars.

Kāppiyārrukkāppiyanār:
on Kalatikāykkanni Nārmuticcēral
Patirruppattu 35

A King's Last Words,

in jail, before he takes his life
If a child of my clan should die,
if it is born dead,
a mere gob of flesh
not yet human,
they will put it to the sword,
to give the thing
a warrior's death.
Will such kings
bring a son into this world
to be kept now
like a dog at the end of a chain,
who must beg,
because of a fire in the belly,
for a drop of water,
and lap up a beggar's drink
brought by jailers,
friends who are not friends?

Cēramān Kanaikkāl Irumporai
Puranānūru 74

The Horse Did Not Come Back

The horse did not come back,
his horse did not come back.
All the other horses have come back.
The horse
of our good man,
who was father in our house
to a little son
with a tuft of hair
like a plume on a steed,
it did not come back.

Has it fallen now,
his horse
that bore him through battle,
has it fallen
like the great tree
standing at the meeting place
of two rivers?

Erumai Veliyanar
Puranānūru 273

King Killi in Combat

With the festival hour close at hand,
his woman in labor,
a sun setting behind pouring rains,
the needle in the cobbler's hand
is in a frenzy
stitching thongs for a cot:
swifter, far swifter,
were the tackles of our lord
wearing garlands of laburnum,
as he wrestled with the enemy
come all the way
to take the land.

Cāttantaiyār:
on Pōrvaikkōpperunar Killi
Puranānūru 82

Religious Poem

Tirumāl

In fire, you are the heat.
In flowers, you are the scent.
Among stones, you are the diamond.
In words, you are truth.
Among virtues, you are love.
In a warrior's wrath, you are the strength.
In the Vedas, you are the secret.
Of the elements, you are the first.
In the scorching sun, you are the light.

In the moonlight, you are the softness.
Everything, you are everything,
the sense, the substance, of everything.

Katuvan Ilaveyinanār
Paripātal 3, lines 63–68

✧ Mahāvamsa ✧

The *Mahāvamsa* (great lineage) is a remarkable Buddhist chronicle; it outlines the history of Buddhism and its establishment in Sri Lanka from the time of the Buddha—a millennium before it was written—to the early fourth century. Based on earlier texts, it contains the earliest written accounts of the life of the Buddha, the spread of Buddhism in India and Sri Lanka, and the origins of the Sinhalese state in Sri Lanka. It combines magical elements, legend, and extraordinarily precise historical data; much of the latter has been corroborated by archaeological evidence.

The *Mahāvamsa* was based on earlier texts, most of them lost, and was put into its final form by the Buddhist monk Mahanama in the early sixth century. It is a work of brilliant scholarship with few parallels worldwide, and it contains historical details, such as the career of the Indian emperor Ashoka, that were centuries old and half a continent away at the time they were recorded. On the other hand, it is a partisan account that emphasizes the Mahāvihara monastic order, the Theravāda school as practiced by that order, and the relationship of that community of monks (*sangha*) with the kings. There were at least a dozen monasteries in Anurādhapura; some of these looked to the Mahāvihara but others did not. It is likely that the lost texts would tell the story differently. The story it tells has been embellished and reinterpreted many times since then, and what passes as the "*Mahāvamsa* version" of Lankan history today is very much a product of these later accretions. Some Lankan Buddhists consider the *Mahāvamsa* to contain revealed truth, and they accept even the mythical sections as true.

The *Mahāvamsa* begins by establishing the magical connections of the Buddha with Sri Lanka and the direct connection of the island with the evolution of Buddhism. Chapters 5 through 10 discuss the founding of the Sinhalese state by Prince Vijāya, descended from a lion (*siha*, from which is derived the name *sihala* for the Sinhalese). The remainder of the *Mahāvamsa* concentrates on two kings, Devānampiyatissa (250–210 BCE Chapters 11–20) and Duṭṭhagāmani (161–137 BCE, Chapters 21–32). The four centuries after the death of Gāmani are treated briefly, usually just listing the extent to which the kings promoted the Buddha's teachings and patronized the *sangha*.

The crucial event is the "third council" at which Buddhists met to establish correct doctrine and the conversion of Devānampiyatissa to Buddhism. According to the *Mahāvamsa*, the purified doctrine decided at the third council was transmitted to Sri Lanka by Ashoka's son Mahinda, who converted the king. The Theravāda Buddhism professed by the Mahāvihara monks thus claimed to be the authentic doctrines of the Buddha. It survived in Sri Lanka as Hinduism, and then Islam displaced Buddhism throughout India and spread from Sri Lanka to Burma and Thailand. Other Buddhists in Nepal, Tibet, China, Korea, and Japan doubt the existence of the third council.

The epic story of Duṭṭhagāmani concerns the unification of the island under a Sinhalese king. Devānampiyatissa ruled at Anurādhapura, but others ruled many small principalities throughout the island, and for much of the following century Tamil rulers of south Indian origin held Anurādhapura. Devānampiyatissa's brother's descendants ruled at Rohaṇa in the southeast of the island. The ruler Kākavaṇṇatissa married Vihāradevī, a daughter of the King of Kalyāṇī in the southwestern part of the island. Their son Duṭṭhagāmani defeated the greatest of the Tamil rulers, Eḷāra, as described in this excerpt.

The story of Duṭṭhagāmani and Eḷāra was centuries old at the time it was written down; the *Mahāvamsa* later shows that there were both Tamil rulers and political fragmentation in Sri Lanka after the events it describes. It was also written at a time that resurgent Hindu kings in south India threatened the Sinhalese, which may have influenced the tone of the account.

British colonial rulers discovered the *Mahāvamsa* and other historical texts in the nineteenth century and set about constructing a history from them. Based on their ideas of race, they regarded this text as an example of warfare between the Buddhist "Aryan" Sinhalese race and the Hindu "Dravidian" Tamil race. In the twentieth century Sinhalese nationalists appropriated much of the colonial framework in viewing the story of Duṭṭhagāmani and Eḷāra as the story of the Sinhalese conquest of the island against Tamil invaders.

The ancient sites of Sri Lanka were abandoned for centuries and excavations were begun only in the nineteenth century. Early photographs of these sites are available at http://www.imagesofceylon.com/index.htm.

Questions

1. What elements in this narrative seem to form its historical core? What elements are clearly implausible?
2. What is the attitude of the author toward king Eḷāra? Can you distinguish between his attitude toward Tamils in general and toward non-Buddhists?
3. This story was repeated frequently during the thirty-year war of the government of Sri Lanka against Tamil separatists that ended in May 2009. In what ways do you think this text could have influenced the conduct of that war?

Mahāvamsa

Wilhelm Geiger, trans., *Mahāvamsa: The Great Chronicle of Ceylon* (Colombo: Ceylon Government Printer, 1912), pp. 143–144, 146, 149–151, 153–154, 170–171, 174–175, 177–178

Chapter 21. The Five Kings

21:13–14. A Damiḷa of noble descent, named Eḷāra, who came hither from the Chola-country to seize on the kingdom, ruled when he had overpowered king Asela, forty-four years, with even justice toward friend and foe, on occasions of disputes at law.

21:15–18. At the head of his bed he had a bell hung up with a long rope so that those who desired a judgement at law might ring it. The king had only one son and one daughter. When once the son of the ruler was going in a car to the Tissa-tank [giant reservoir], he killed unintentionally a young calf lying on the road with the mother cow, by driving the wheel over its neck. The cow came and dragged at the bell in bitterness of heart; and the king caused his son's head to be severed (from his body) with that same wheel. . . .

21:21–26. When the king, who was a protector of tradition, albeit he knew not the peerless virtues of the most precious of the three gems, was going (once) to the Cetiya-mountain to invite the brotherhood of bhikkhus, he caused, as he arrived upon a car, with the point of the yoke on the waggon, an injury to the thūpa [dagoba; large domed reliquary] of the Conqueror at a (certain) spot. The ministers said to him: "King, the thūpa has been injured by thee." Though this had come to pass without his intending it, yet the king leaped from his car and flung himself down upon the road with the words: "Sever my head also (from the trunk) with the wheel." They answered him: "Injury to another does our Master in no wise allow; make thy peace (with the bhikkhus) by restoring the thūpa"; and in order to place (anew) the fifteen stones that had been broken off he spent just fifteen thousand kahapanas. . . .

Chapter 22. The Birth of Prince Gāmani

22.1 WHEN he had slain Eḷāra, Duṭṭhagāmaṇi became king. To show clearly how this came to pass the story in due order (of events) is this:

22.2–6. King Devānampiyatissa's second brother, the vice-regent named Mahanaga, was dear to his brother. The king's consort, that foolish woman, coveted the kingship for her own son and ever nursed the wish to slay the vice-regent . . . the vice-regent, with his wives, men and horses, went, to save his life, to Rohaṇa. . . .

22.42–46. And there came on the virtuous queen [Vihāradevī] these longings of a woman with child. (This) did she crave: that while making a pillow for her head of a honeycomb one usabha long and resting on her left side in her beautiful bed, she should eat the honey that remained when she had given twelve thousand bhikkhus to eat of it; and then she longed to drink (the water) that had served to cleanse the sword with which the head of the first warrior among king Eḷāra's warriors had been struck off, (and she longed to drink it) standing on this very head, and moreover (she longed) to adorn herself with garlands of unfaded lotus-blossoms brought from the lotus-marshes of Anurādhapura.

22.46–47. The queen told this to the king, and the king asked the soothsayers. When the soothsayers heard it they said: "The queen's son, when he has vanquished the Damiḷas and built up a united kingdom, will make the doctrine to shine forth brightly." . . .

22:59–61. In time the queen bore a noble son, endowed with all auspicious signs, and great was the rejoicing in the house of the great monarch. By the effect of his merit there arrived that very day, from this place and that, seven ships laden with manifold gems. And in like manner, by the power of his merit, an elephant of the six-tusked race brought his young one thither and left him here and went his way. [Many other auspicious omens appeared] . . . when it was said to them: "Never will we fight with the Damiḷas; with such thoughts eat ye this portion here," Tissa dashed the food away with his hand, but Gāmaṇi who had (in like manner) flung away the morsel of rice, went to his bed, and drawing in his hands and feet he lay upon his bed. The queen came, and caressing Gāmaṇi spoke thus: "Why dost thou not lie easily upon thy bed with limbs stretched out, my son?" "Over there beyond the Ganga are the Damiḷas, here on this side is the Gotha-ocean, how can I lie with outstretched limbs?" he answered. When the king heard his thoughts he remained silent.

Growing duly Gāmaṇi came to sixteen years, vigorous, renowned, intelligent and a hero in majesty and might.

In this changing existence do beings indeed (only) by works of merit come to such rebirth as they desire; pondering thus the wise man will be ever filled with zeal in the heaping up of meritorious works.

Here ends the twenty-second chapter, called "The Birth of Prince Gāmaṇi," in the Mahāvamsa compiled for the serene joy and emotion of the pious.

Chapter 25. The Victory of Duṭṭhagāmaṇi

25:1–10 WHEN the king Duṭṭhagāmaṇi had provided for his people and had had a relic put into his spear he marched, with chariots, troops and beasts for riders, to Tissamaharama, and when he had shown favour to the brotherhood he said: "I will go on to the land on the further side of the river to bring glory to the doctrine. Give us, that we may treat them with honour, bhikkhus who shall go on with us, since the sight of bhikkhus is blessing and protection for us." As a penance the brotherhood allowed him five hundred ascetics; taking this company of bhikkhus with him the king marched forth, and when he had caused the road in Malaya leading hither to be made ready he mounted the elephant Kandula and, surrounded by his warriors, he took the field with a mighty host. With the one end yet in Mahagama the train of the army reached to Guttahalaka.

Arrived at Mahiyangana he overpowered the Damiḷa Chatta. When he had slain the Damiḷas in that very place he came then to Ambatitthaka, which had a trench leading from the river, and (conquered) the Damiḷa Titthamba; fighting the crafty and powerful foe for four months he (finally) overcame him by cunning, since he placed his mother in his view.

When the mighty man marching thence down (the river) had conquered seven mighty Damiḷa princes in one day and had established peace, he gave over the booty to his troops.

25:57–75 When Eḷāra in full armour had mounted his elephant Mahāpabbata he came thither with chariots, soldiers and beasts for riders. When the battle began the mighty and terrible Dāghajantu seized his sword and shield for battle, and leaping eighteen cubits up into the air and cleaving the effigy of the king with his sword, he scattered the first body of troops. When the mighty (warrior) had in this manner scattered also the other bodies of troops, he charged at the body of troops with which king Gāmaṇi stood. But when he began to attack the king, the mighty warrior Sūranimila insulted him, proclaiming his own name. Dāghajantu thought: "I will slay him," and leaped into the air full of rage. But Sūranimila held the shield toward him as he alighted (in leaping). But Dāghajantu thought: "I will cleave him in twain, together with the shield," and struck the shield with the sword. Then Sūranimila let go the shield. And as he clove (only) the shield thus released Dāghajantu fell there, and Sūranimila, springing up, slew the fallen (man) with his spear. Phussadeva blew his conch shell, the army of the Damiḷas was scattered; nay, Eḷāra turned to flee and they slew many Damiḷas. The water in the tank there was dyed red with the blood of the slain, therefore it was known by the name Kulantavapi.

King Duṭṭhagāmaṇi proclaimed with beat of drum: "None but myself shall slay Eḷāra." When he himself, armed, had mounted the armed elephant Kandula he pursued Eḷāra and came to the south gate (of Anuradhapura).

Near the south gate of the city the two kings fought; Eḷāra hurled his dart, Gāmaõi evaded it; he made his own elephant pierce (Eḷāra's) elephant with his tusks and he hurled his dart at Eḷāra; and this (latter) fell there, with his elephant.

When he had thus been victorious in battle and had united Lanka under one rule he marched, with chariots, troops and beasts for riders, into the capital. In the city he caused the drum to be beaten, and when he had summoned the people from a *yojana* [several miles] around he celebrated the funeral rites for king Eḷāra. On the spot where his body had fallen he burned it with the catafalque, and there did he build a monument and ordain worship. And even to this day the princes of Lanka, when they draw near to this place, are wont to silence their music because of this worship.

When he had thus overpowered thirty-two Damiḷa kings Duṭṭhagāmaṇi ruled over Lanka in single sovereignty.

25:101–116 Sitting then on the terrace of the royal palace, adorned, lighted with fragrant lamps and filled with many a perfume, magnificent with nymphs in the guise of dancing-girls, while he rested on his soft and fair couch, covered with costly draperies, he, looking back upon his glorious victory, great though it was, knew no joy, remembering that thereby was wrought the destruction of millions (of beings).

When the arahants [monks who had attained enlightenment] in Piyangudipa knew his thought they sent eight arahants to comfort the king. And they, coming in the middle watch of the night, alighted at the palace-gate. Making known that they were come thither through the air they mounted to the terrace of the palace.

The great king greeted them, and when he had invited them to be seated and had done them reverence in many ways he asked the reason of their coming. "We are sent by the brotherhood at Piyangudipa to comfort thee, O lord of men."

And thereon the king said again to them: "How shall there be any comfort for me, O venerable sirs, since by me was caused the slaughter of a great host numbering millions?"

"From this deed arises no hindrance in thy way to heaven. Only one and a half human beings have been slain here by thee, O lord of men. The one had come unto the (three) refuges, the other had taken on himself the five precepts. Unbelievers and men of evil life were the rest, not more to be esteemed than beasts. But as for thee, thou wilt bring glory to the doctrine of the Buddha in manifold ways; therefore cast away care from thy heart, O ruler of men!"

Thus exhorted by them the great king took comfort. When he had bidden them farewell and had given them leave to depart he lay down again and thought: "Without the brotherhood you shall never take a meal, thus our mother and father have caused to swear us in our boyhood at the meal. Have I ever eaten anything whatsoever without giving to the brotherhood of bhikkhus?" Then he saw that he had, all unthinkingly, eaten pepper in the pod, at the morning meal, leaving none for the brotherhood; and he thought: "For this I must do penance."

Should a man think on the hosts of human beings murdered for greed in countless myriads, and should he carefully keep in mind the evil (arising from that), and should he also very carefully keep in mind the mortality as being the murderer of all, then will he, in this way, shortly win freedom from suffering and a happy condition.

Here ends the twenty-fifth chapter, called "The Victory of Duṭṭhagāmaṇi in the Mahāvamsa, compiled for the serene joy and emotion of the pious.

✧ The Perfect Bride ✧

Dandin

The Perfect Bride is one of an impressive collection of Sanskrit romances dating from the fifth to the seventh centuries. These tales are set in the time of the Gupta Empire (c. 320–550), an era in which Indian civilization reached great political and cultural heights. When the Kushan Empire, with its capital at Peshawar, collapsed, the ensuing power vacuum in northern India was slowly occupied by the rulers of the small state who claimed descent from the Guptan rulers of the Mauryan Empire (322–185 BCE). The founder of this new dynasty took the name Chandragupta I (r. 320–298 CE) and began to expand his power to the north and west. By the reign of Chandragupta II (r.c. 380–413 CE), the empire extended across northern India from the mouth of the Ganges to the Arabian Sea.

It was an age of prosperity, in which Indian merchants dominated the seas and carried Indian commerce and culture into Southeast Asia, Indonesia, and elsewhere along the littoral of the Indian Ocean. At the same time, Buddhist missionaries carried Indian religion, philosophy, and art overland to the north and east. Culture flourished, and Indian literature and art reached heights that set the standard for centuries to come.

During this period, a great revival occurred in the Sanskrit language. It again became a living and literary language, in which secular works of great sophistication were composed. Guptan literature was vibrant and dynamic, excelling in such varied forms as the fable, lyric poetry, drama, and romance. In all, the emphasis was less on the warrior or king than on the merchant and traveler. The three most popular themes were the pursuit of profit, virtue, and love.

The three great writers of narrative prose during the period are generally considered to be Subandhu, Dandin, and Bana, roughly contemporary during the late sixth and early seventh centuries. *The Perfect Bride* is taken from Dandin's *Tales of Ten Princes*, a fascinating collection of sometimes humorous and often scandalous stories. These tales are particularly interesting for the relatively realistic view they present of the life of the times. During their adventures, the ten princes encounter a virtual cross-section of Guptan society, including thieves, princesses, prostitutes, and peasants.

The leading characters of *The Perfect Bride* are Saktikumara, the son of a merchant prince, and a young girl who becomes the object of his romantic interest. The story revolves around Saktikumara's desire for a bride who is not only physically attractive, but possesses "all the wifely virtues." He puts the young woman to a difficult test, which she ingeniously passes. Content that he has found a woman possessing all the qualities he desires, he marries her and then, of course, begins to take her for granted. The story ends with Saktikumara, finally won over by his wife's qualities, abandoning his shameful ways and adopting a more virtuous way of life.

Questions

1. What are the virtues Saktikumara seeks in a wife? Do you consider these valid?
2. What do the "markings" that he looks for signify?
3. What qualities does Saktikumara's test seek to discover, and how?
4. On the basis of *The Perfect Bride*, discuss the role of women in medieval Indian society.

The Perfect Bride

J.A.B. van Buitenen, trans., *Tales of Ancient India* (Chicago: University of Chicago Press, 1959), pp. 157–160

In Tamil Land in a city called Kanci lived the millionaire son of a merchant prince. His name was Saktikumara, and when he was about eighteen years old, he began to worry.

"There is no happiness without a wife," he reflected, "nor with a wife if she is disagreeable. But how to find a wife who has all the wifely virtues?" Distrusting the purely accidental aspect of marriage with a wife taken at the recommendation of others, he became an astrologer and palmist and, tucking two pounds of unthreshed rice in the hem of his garment, wandered through the land. Everyone who had daughters displayed them before him, saying "Here is a fortune teller!" But however well marked and suitable the girl was, Saktikumara would ask, "Are you able, my dear, to prepare a complete meal for us with these two pounds of rice?" Thus, he roamed from house to house, entering only to be laughed at and thrown out.

One day, in a hamlet on the southern bank of the Kaveri in Sibi country, an ayah showed him a young girl with but a few jewels, who, together with her parents, had gone through a large fortune of which only a decrepit house was left. He stared at her.

"Here is a girl," he thought, "with a perfectly proportioned figure—not too heavy, not too thin, neither too short nor too tall—with regular features and a fair complexion. Her toes are pink inside; the soles are marked with auspicious lines, of barley grain, fish, lotus, and pitcher; her ankles are symmetrical and the feet well rounded and not muscular. The calves are perfectly curved, and the knees are hardly noticeable, as though they were swallowed by the sturdy thighs. The loin dimples are precisely parallel and square and shed lustre upon buttocks round as chariot wheels. Her abdomen is adorned by three folds and is slender around the deep navel, even a little caved. The broad-based breasts with proud nipples fill the full region of her chest. Her copper-red fingers, straight and well rounded, with long, smooth, polished nails like glistening gems, adorn hands which show the happy signs of abundance of grain, wealth, and sons. Her arms, which start from sloping shoulders and taper to the wrists, are very delicate. Her slender neck is curved and bent like a seashell. Her lotus-like face shows unblemished red lips that are rounded in the middle, a lovely and unabbreviated chin, firm but fully rounded cheeks, dark brows that arch a little but do not meet, and a nose like a haughty Sesamum blossom. The wide eyes, jet black, dazzling white, and reddish brown, are radiant and tender and profound and languidly roving. Her forehead is shapely like the crescent moon, her locks darkly alluring like a mine of sapphires. The long ears are twice adorned, by a fading lotus and a playful stalk. Her long, abundant, and fragrant locks are glossy black, every single hair of them, and do not fade to brown even at the ends. When her figure is so beautiful, her character cannot be different. My heart goes out to her. However, I shall not marry her before I have tried her: for those who act without circumspection inevitably reap repentance in abundance." So he asked with a kindly look, "Would you be able, my dear, to make me a complete meal with this rice?"

The girl gave her old servant a meaningful glance; whereupon the woman took the two pounds of rice from him and placed it on the terrace before the door after sprinkling and scrubbing it thoroughly. Then she washed the girl's feet. The girl then dried the sweet-smelling rice measure by measure, repeatedly turning it over in the sun, and when it was thoroughly dry, she spread it on a hard, smooth part of the floor, threshed it very, very gently with the edge of a reed-stalk, and finally took all the rice grains out of the husks without breaking them. Then she said to her ayah: "Mother, jewelers want these husks; they use them to polish jewelry. Sell it to them and, with the pennies they give you, you must buy good hard firewood sticks, neither too dry nor too damp, a small-sized pan, and two shallow bowls."

When the servant had done that, the girl placed the rice grains in a shallow mortar of kakubha wood with a flat, wide bottom and began pounding them with a long, heavy, iron-tipped, smooth-bodied pestle of khadira wood that was slightly recessed in the middle to form a grip. She tired her arms in a charming play of raising and dropping, picking up and picking out single grains, which she then cleaned of chaff and awn in a winnowing basket, washed repeatedly in water, and, after a small offering to the fireplace, dropped in boiling water, five parts water to one part rice.

As the grains softened and started to jump and swelled to the size of a bud, she lowered the fire and, holding the lid on the pot, poured out the scum. Then she plunged her spoon in the rice, turned the grains with the spoon, and, having satisfied herself that they were evenly boiled, turned the pot upside down on its lid to let the rice steam. She poured water over those firesticks which had not burned up entirely, and when the fire had died and the heat was gone, she sent this charcoal to the dealers: "Buy with the coin you receive as much of vegetables, ghee, curds, oil, myrobalan [dried medicinal fruit], and tamarinds as you can get."

When this had been done, she added two or three kinds of spices, and once the rice broth was transferred to a new bowl placed on wet sand, she cooled it with gentle strokes of a palmleaf fan, added salt, and scented it with fragrant smoke. Then she ground the myrobalan to a fine lotus-sweet powder, and finally relayed through her servant the invitation to a bath. The old nurse, clean from a bath herself, gave Saktikumara myrobalan and oil, whereupon he bathed. After his bath he sat down on a plank placed on sprinkled and swept stones. He touched the two bowls that were placed on a light, green banana-tree leaf from her own garden—a quarter of one leaf was used—and she set the rice broth before him. He drank it and, feeling happy and content after his journey, let a sweet lassitude pervade his body. Then she served him two spoonfuls of rice porridge and added a serving of butter, soup, and condiment. Finally, she served him the remaining boiled rice with curds mixed with mace, cardamom, and cinnamon, and fragrant cool buttermilk and fermented rice gruel. He finished all the rice and side dishes. Then he asked for water. From a new pitcher with water that was scented with the incense of aloe wood, permeated with the fragrance of fresh Bignonia blossoms and perfumed with lotus buds, she poured out an even thin stream. He held his mouth close to the vessel; and while the snow-cold spattering drops bristled and reddened his eyelashes, his ears rejoiced in the tinkling sound of the stream, his cheeks tickled and thrilled at the pleasurable touch, his nostrils opened to the fragrance of the lotus buds, and his sense of taste delighted in the delicious flavor, he drank the water to his heart's content. With a nod of his head he indicated that she stop pouring, and she gave him, from another vessel, fresh water to rinse his mouth. When the old woman had removed the scraps of the meal and had cleaned the stone floor with yellow cowdung, he spread his ragged upper cloth on the ground and took a short nap.

Highly satisfied, he married the girl with proper rites and took her with him. Once he had brought her home, he ignored her and wooed a courtesan; the bride treated even that woman as her dear friend. She waited on her husband as if he were a god, untiringly. She did the household chores without fail and, wonder of tact, won the affection of the servants. Conquered by her virtues, her husband put the entire household in her charge and, depending body and soul on her alone, applied himself to the pursuit of Virtue, Wealth, and Love. Thus, I say, a wife's virtue is a man's happiness.

✧ Gitagovinda ✧

Jayadeva

Classical India was a land of great linguistic and political diversity, united by what anthropologists call the "great tradition." This consisted of the high philosophical concepts, rituals, and mythology of Hinduism; the literary culture of the royal courts; the laws of the Brahmans; and the practices and customs of learned Brahmans themselves, which formed a model of behavior for the rest of society. The "little tradition" of village life, within which the great mass of the Indian population lived out their lives, encompassed the close interrelationships of family and friends, the familiarity with the fields and orchards, the cycle of seasons with their festivals of fertility and thanksgiving, and a general sense of harmony with the world of nature. Local customs and traditions dominated Indian daily life, and Brahman families living within the village community linked the peasants with the great tradition. It was the combination of these two traditions that gave Indian culture the unity and continuity it would not otherwise have possessed. One of the important factors joining the great and little traditions was their common devotion to the great god Vishnu, in his earth-dwelling form of Krishna.

Vishnu appears in the Rig Veda only as the dwarf who measured the earth in three strides. In later centuries, this dwarf was considered to have been only one of Vishnu's ten avatars (incarnations), for Vishnu was a god who visited the earth. Some of these incarnations, such as Rama (of the epic poem *The Ramayana*) and Krishna, were probably heroic warrior-kings famed in legend long before they came to be identified as personifications of Vishnu.

By the seventh century, Vishnu began to gain greater importance in Indian religion. Hindu devotionalism came to be expressed in terms of a reciprocal love between the worshipper and the god, and the acceptance of this concept by the Brahmans gave India a worship in which all could join as individuals and equals. Of the ten avatars of Vishnu described here, none was more beloved to the Indians than the fun-loving and ardent Krishna.

The life and deeds of Krishna are the theme of many myths and legends, from his birth and mischievous childhood to his role as the awesome charioteer in the *Bhagavad Gita*. In the tenth-century *Bhagavata Purana*, the most popular of the eighteen Sanskrit *puranas*, he appears in the form of a cowherd (*govinda*). In this tale, the young Krishna flirts and sports with a group of pretty cowherdesses (*gopi*), finally falling in love with Radha, one of their number. By the time of the *Gitagovinda*, the cow had come to symbolize maternal love and the spirit of devotion to Krishna. In the *Gitagovinda*, Jayadeva explains through myth why this came to be.

In the West, the *Gitagovinda* has been criticized for its openly erotic character, but in India it remains one of the central works of devotion to Vishnu. It draws not only on earlier devotional literature, but also on Tantric ritual, the character of which is amply illustrated by the erotic themes in temple sculpture of the period. For the Indians of the time, it was only reasonable to describe abstract concepts in concrete terms through allegory. It seemed perfectly natural to them to describe their joyous love for their god in terms of the most ecstatic physical pleasure they knew.

The excerpts in this Victorian translation come from the beginning and near the end of the poem. The first excerpt is from Jayadeva's invocation and hymn to Vishnu, after which the narrative begins with Radha's description of how she observed Krishna's lovemaking with the other *gopis*. She hides in anger and jealousy; Krishna, realizing his love for Radha, searches unsuccessfully for her. He then waits for Radha to come to him. Radha wastes away from the anguish of separation and from the thought that Krishna no longer cares for her. Radha's maid passes back and forth between the two, describing the agony of the one to the other and urging each to overcome pride and to take the first step toward reconciliation. After a night and a day of separation, it is Krishna who comes to Radha and declares his love. He then returns to his home in the forest; Radha follows him to his hut.

Edwin Arnold prudishly omits the explicit love play that concludes the poem. Jayadeva stresses the cosmic significance of the relationship by referring to Krishna by various names that invoke Hindu mythology: Madhava (descendant of Madhu, or Spring), Hari (a demon), Narayana, and Yadu or Yadava (hero). Radha is called Sri, "radiance" or "beauty," which is another name of the goddess Lakshmi, consort of Vishnu. To peasant worshippers, the allegory was clear; after a winter of short days, cold winds, and perhaps diminishing supplies of food, the god Vishnu arrives as Spring, a hero defeating death and Winter, and, with joy and love, blesses humankind with the fruits of the season to come.

Illustrations from this work have been a favorite of Indian artists for centuries and are widely available on the Internet, many of them on the websites of art dealers.

Questions

1. What does Jayadeva say (given in italics) are his motives for composing this work?
2. Some people claim that uninhibited eroticism, such as that demonstrated in the *Gitagovinda*, is a sign of decline in a civilization. What evidence for and against this argument can you find in this example?
3. The *Gitagovinda* is written in an ornate Sanskrit understood by few people, yet it was intended to be sung and danced publicly. How might ordinary Hindus have interpreted the story?

Gitagovinda

Edwin Arnold, *Poems* (Boston: Little, Brown, 1910), pp. 1–5, 9–14, 79–87

Introduction

The sky is clouded; and the wood resembles
The sky, thick arched with black tamala boughs;
"Oh Radha, Radha! Take this soul that trembles

In life's deep midnight, to thy Golden house."
So Nanda spoke—and led by Radha's spirit,
The feet of Krishna found the road aright;
Wherefore, in bliss which all high hearts inherit,
Together taste they love's divine delight.

He who wrote these things for thee,
Of the son of Wassoodee,
Was the poet Jayadeva,
Him Saraswati gave ever
Fancies fair his mind to throng,
Like pictures palace-walls along;
Ever to his notes of love
Lakshmi's mystic dancers move.
If thy spirit seeks to brood
On Hari glorious, Hari good;
If it feeds on solemn numbers
Dim as dreams and soft as slumbers,
Lend thine ear to Jayadev,
Lord of all spells that save.
Umapatidhara's strain
Glows like roses after rain;
Sharan's stream like song is grand,
If it is tide ye understand;
Bard more wise beneath the sun
Is not found than Govardhun;
Doyi holds the listener still
With his slokes [verses] of subtle skill;
But for sweet words suited well
Jayadeva doth excel.

Hymn to Vishnu

Oh thou that held'st the blessed Veda dry
When all things else beneath the floods were hurled;
Strong Fish God! Ark of men! *Jai!* Hari, *jai!*
Hail, Keshav, hail! Thou master of the world!

The round world rested on thy spacious nape;
Upon thy neck, like a mere mole, it is stood:
Oh thou that took'st for us the tortoise shape,
Hail, Keshav, hail! Ruler of wave and wood!

The world upon thy curving tusk sate sure,
Like the Moon's dark disk in her crescent pale;
Oh thou who didst for us assume the boar,
Immortal Conqueror! Hail, Keshav, hail!

When thou thy Giant-Foe did seize and rend,
Fierce, fearful, long, and sharp were fang and nail.
Thou who Lion and the man didst blend,
Lord of the Universe! Hail, Narsingh, hail!

Wonderful Dwarf!—who with a threefold stride
Cheated king Bali—where thy footsteps fall
Men's sins, O Wamuna! are set aside:
O Keshav, hail! Thou help and hope of all!

The sins of this sad earth thou didst assoil,
The anguish of its creatures thou didst heal;
Freed are we from all terrors by thy toil:
Hail, Purshuram, hail! Lord of the biting steel!

To thee the fell Ten-Headed yielded life.
Thou in dread battle laid'st the monster low!
Ah Rama! Dear to Gods and men that strife;
We praise thee, Master of the Matchless bow!

With clouds for garments glorious thou dost fare,
Veiling thy dazzling majesty and might,
As when Yamuna saw thee with the share,
A peasant—yet the King of Day and Night.

Merciful-Hearted! When thou camest as Boodh [Buddha]—
Albeit 'twas written in the Scriptures so—
Thou bad'st our altars be no more imbrued
With blood of victims: Keshav! bending low—

We praise thee, Wielder of the sweeping sword,
Brilliant as curving comets in the gloom,
Whose edge shall smite the fierce barbarian horde;
Hail to thee, Keshav! Hail, and hear, and come.

1. The Sports of Krishna

Beautiful Radha, jasmine-bosomed Radha,
All in the Spring-time waited by the wood
For Krishna fair, Krishna the all-forgetful,—
Krishna with earthly love's false fire consuming
And some one of her maidens sang this song:—

I know where Krishna tarries in these early days of Spring,
When every wind from warm Malay brings fragrance on its wing;
Brings fragrance stolen far away from thickets of the clove,
In jungles where the bees hum and the Koil [cuckoo] flutes her love;
He dances with the dancers, at the merry morrice one,
All in the budding Spring-time, for 'tis sad to be alone.

I know how Krishna passes these hours of blue and gold,
When parted lovers sigh to meet and greet and closely hold
Hand fast in hand; and every branch upon the Valkul-tree
Droops downward with a hundred blooms, in every bloom a bee;
He is dancing with the dancers to a laughter-moving tone,
In the soft awakening Spring-time, when 'tis hard to live alone.

When Kroona-flowers, that open at a lover's lightest tread,
Break, and, for shame at what they hear, from white blush\ modest red;
And all the spears on all the boughs of all the Ketuk-glades
Seem ready darts to pierce the hearts of wandering youths and maids;
'Tis there thy Krishna dances till the merry drum is done,
All in the sunny Spring-time, when who can live alone?

Where the breaking forth of blossom on the yellow Keshra-sprays
Dazzles like Kama's sceptre, whom all the world obeys;
And Patal-buds fill drowsy bees from pink delicious bowls,
As Kama's nectared goblet steeps in languor human souls;
There he dances with the dancers, and of Radha thinketh none,
All in the warm new Spring-tide, when none will live alone.

Where the breath of waving Madhvi pours incense through the
grove,
And silken Mogras lull the sense with essences of love,—
The silken-soft pale Mogra, whose perfume fine and faint
Can melt the coldness of a maid, the sternness of a saint—
There dances with those dancers thine other self, thine Own;
All in the languorous Spring-time, when none will live alone.

Where—as if warm lips torched sealed eyes and waked them—
all in bloom
Opens upon the mangoes to feel the sunshine come;
And Atimuktas wind their arms of softest green about,
Clasping the stems, while calm and clear great Jumna spreadeth
out;
There dances and there laughs thy Love, with damsels many
an one,
In the rosy days of Spring-Time, for he will not live alone.

Mark this song of Jayadev!
Deep as pearl in ocean-wave
Lurketh in its lines a wonder
Which the wise alone will ponder:
Though it seemeth of the Earth,
Heavenly is the music's birth;
Telling darkly of delights
In the wood, of wasted nights,
Of witless days, and fruitless love,
And false pleasures of the grove,
And rash passions of the prime,
And those dances of Spring-time;
Time, which seems so subtle-sweet,
Time, which pipes to dancing-feet,
Ah! So softly—Ah! So sweetly—
That among those wood-maids featly
Krishna cannot choose but dance,
Letting pass life's greater chance.

Yet the winds that sigh so
As they stir the rose,
Wake a sigh from Krishna
Wistfuller than those;

All their faint breaths swinging
The creepers to and fro
Pass like rustling arrows
Shot from Kama's bow:
Thus among the dancers
What those Zephyrs bring
Strikes to Krishna's spirit
Like a darted sting.

And as if—far wandered—
The traveller should hear
The bird of home, the Koil,
With nest-notes rich and clear;
And there should come one moment
A blessed fleeting dream
Of the bees among the mangoes
Beside his native stream;
So flash those sudden yearnings,
That sense of a dearer thing,
The love and lack of Radha
Upon his soul in spring.

9. The End of Krishna's Trial

Yet not quite did the doubts of Radha die,
Nor her sweet brows unbend; but she, the Maid—
Knowing her heart so tender, her soft arms
Aching to take him in, her rich mouth sad
For the comfort of his kiss, and these fears false—
Spake yet a little in fair words like these,

The lesson that thy faithful love has taught him
He has heard;
The wind of spring, obeying thee, hath brought him
At thy word;
What joy in all the three worlds was so precious
To thy mind?
My proud one! do not indulge in scorn
Ah, be kind!

No longer from his earnest eyes conceal
Thy delights;
Lift thy face, and let the jealous veil reveal
All his rights;
The glory of thy beauty was but given
For content
My proud one! do not indulge in scorn
Oh, relent!

Remember, being distant, how he bore thee
In his heart;
Look on him sadly turning from before thee
To depart;
Is he not the soul thou lovedst, sitting lonely
In the wood?
My proud one! do not indulge in scorn
'Tis not good!

He who grants thee high delight in bridal-bower
Pardons long;
What the gods do love may do at such an hour
Without wrong;
Why weepest thou? why keepest thou in anger
Thy lashes down?
My proud one! do not indulge in scorn
Do not frown!

Lift thine eyes now, and look on him, bestowing,
Without speech;
Let him pluck at last the flower so sweetly growing
In his reach;
The fruit of lips, of loving tones, of glances
That forgive;
My proud one! do not indulge in scorn
Let him live!

Let him speak with thee, and pray to thee, and prove thee
All his truth;
Let his silent loving lamentation move thee
Asking truth;
How knowest thou? Ah, listen, dearest Lady,
He is there;

My proud one! do not indulge in scorn
Thou must hear!

O rare voice, which is a spell
Unto all on earth who dwell!
O rich voice of rapturous love,
Making melody above!
Krishna's, Hari's—one in two,
Sound these mortal verses through!
Sound like that soft flute which made
Such a magic in the shade—
Calling deer-eyed maidens nigh,
Waking wish and stirring sigh,
Thrilling blood and melting breasts,
Whispering love's divine unrests,
Winning blessings to descend,
Bringing earthly ills to end;—
Be thou heard in this song now
Thou, the great Enchantment, thou!

10. Krishna in Paradise

But she, abasing still her glorious eyes,
And still not yielding all her face to him,
Relented, till with softer upturned look
She smiled, while the Maid pleaded so thereat
Came Krishna nearer, and his eager lips
Mixed sighs with words in this fond song he sang,

O angel of my hope! O my heart's home!
My fear is lost in love, my love in fear;
This bids me trust my burning wish, and come,
That checks me with its memories, drawing near:
Lift up thy look, and let the thing it saith
End fear with grace, or darken love to death.

Or only speak once more, for though thou slay me,
Thy heavenly mouth must move, and I shall hear
Dulcet delights of perfect music sway me
Again—again that voice so blest and dear;
Sweet Judge! the prisoner prayeth for his doom
That he may hear his fate divinely come.

Speak once more! then thou canst not choose but show
Thy mouth's unparalleled and honeyed wonder
Where, like pearls hid in red-lipped shells, the row
Of pearly teeth thy rose-red lips lie under;
Ah me! I am that bird that woos the moon,
And pipes—poor fool! to make it glitter soon.

Yet hear me on—because I cannot stay
The passion of my soul, because my gladness
Will pour forth from my heart,—since that far day
When through the mist of all my sin and sadness
Thou didst vouchsafe—Surpassing One!—to break,
All else I slighted for thy noblest sake.

Thou, thou hast been my blood, my breath, my being;
The pearl to plunge for in the sea of life;
The sight to strain for, past the bounds of seeing;
The victory to win through longest strife;
My Queen! my crowned Mistress! my sphered bride!
Take this for truth, that what I say beside

Of bold love—grown full-orbed at sight of thee—
May be forgiven with a quick remission;
For, thou divine fulfilment of all hope!
Thou all-undreamed completion of the vision!
I gaze upon thy beauty, and my fear
Passes as clouds do, when the moon shines clear.

So if thou'rt angry still, this shall avail,
Look straight at me, and let thy bright glance wound me;
Fetter me! gyve me! lock me in the gaol
Of thy delicious arms; make fast around me
The silk-soft manacles of wrists and hands,
Then kill me! I shall never break those bands.

The starlight jewels flashing on thy breast
Have not my right to hear thy beating heart;
The happy jasmine-buds that clasp thy waist
Are soft usurpers of my place and part;
If that fair girdle only there must shine,
Give me the girdle's life—the girdle mine!

Thy brow like smooth Bandhuka-leaves; thy cheek
Which the dark-tinted Madhuk's velvet shows;
Thy long-lashed Lotus eyes, lustrous and meek;
Thy nose a Tila-bud; thy teeth like rows
Of Kunda-petals! he who pierceth hearts
Points with thy lovelinesses all five darts.

But Radiant, Perfect, Sweet, Supreme, forgive!
My heart is wise—my tongue is foolish still:
I know where I am come—I know I live—
I know that thou art Radha—that this will
Last and be heaven: that I have leave to rise
Up from thy feet, and look into thine eyes!

And, nearer coming, I ask for grace
Now that the blest eyes turn to mine;
Faithful I stand in this sacred place
Since first I saw them shine:
Dearest glory that stills my voice,
Beauty unseen, unknown, unthought
Splendor of love, in whose sweet light
Darkness is past and nought;
Ah, beyond words that sound on earth,
Golden bloom of the garden of heaven
Radha, enchantress! Radha, the queen!
Be this trespass forgiven—
In that I dare, with courage too much
And a heart afraid,—so bold it is grown—
To hold thy hand with a bridegroom's touch,
And take thee for mine, mine own.

So they met and so they ended
Pain and parting, being blended
Life with life—made one for ever
In high love; and Jayadeva
Hasteneth on to close the story
Of their bridal grace and glory.

✧ Songs of Kabir ✧

The violence that often erupted between the Muslim and Hindu inhabitants of India in the course of the nineteenth and twentieth centuries gave their British colonial administrators the general impression that the two religions were simply incompatible and that hostile relations between them were inevitable. Certainly this was true in recent times. At the point of achieving their dream of an independent India, the Muslim and Hindu leaders of the national movement each found that they simply did not trust each other enough to face the prospect of possibly being governed by members of the other sect. The result was the partitioning of India in 1947 into a Hindu India and a Muslim Pakistan, and the mass migration of millions of people from one nation to the other, a migration that was marked by scenes of incredible hatred and savagery between groups of Muslim and Hindu refugees. Such had not always been the case, however; at times in the past, Muslims and Hindus had lived together in relative peace.

In 1192, Hindu armies were decisively defeated by Muslim invaders at the battle of Taraori in north India. The Muslims went on to conquer Delhi, from which they ruled much of India for the next three centuries (1206–1526). In this period, north India became known to Muslims as Dar al-Islam (Abode of Islam), rather than by its former name of Dar al-Harb (Abode of War).

These Indian Muslims were far removed from Islam's Arabic origins, however. The rulers of the Delhi Sultanate were of Turkish descent and were heavily influenced by a rich and sophisticated Persian culture that antedated Islam by 1,000 years and more. They formed a tiny minority in densely populated India, so that Islamic law could not be enforced rigidly, and the sultans began compromising early. The Muslim rulers generally tried to avoid alienating the Hindu majority, although some religious zealots took delight in destroying ancient temples and sculptures and in attempting to force the Hindus to convert to Islam. Hindus successfully resisted these efforts and preserved their traditional beliefs for many of the same reasons that the Chinese of the same period were successfully resisting the foreign influence of their alien Mongol rulers.

Individual Indians would have found it difficult to convert to Islam even if they were truly won over to Muslim spiritual ideals. Hindu converts lost their standing in family, caste, and village, and so, when conversion to Islam did take place, it was as a collective phenomenon. Such conversions tended to concentrate along the periphery of Muslim territories—Baluchistan, Sind, Kashmir, and western Punjab, areas that later became Pakistan, and, above all, Bengal, now the Muslim nation of Bangladesh. On the other hand, some Muslims began adopting Hindu religious customs, incorporating music and dance, local shrines, and local legends into their worship. On the social level, some groups of Muslims began acting like castes—making great distinctions between *Ashraf* (immigrants) or Muslims by birth and *Ajlaf* (converts to the faith).

The period of the Delhi Sultanate saw the resurgence of devotional Hinduism. It must be remembered that this was the same era in which Jayadeva wrote the *Gitagovinda*, one of the great expressions of popular devotion to Krishna and adoration of Vishnu, whose symbol he was. The ascetic and mystical Islamic movement known as Sufism also believed in a god of love and in the personal ecstasy to be found in loving that god in return. With such basic convictions in common, it is not surprising that some sought to integrate these Hindu and Muslim beliefs into an adoration of the one true god of all. Muslim poet-saints began to express their devotion in songs written in native Indian languages, particularly Tamil in the south and Hindi in the north.

Kabir (c. 1440–1518) is one of the most famous of these poet-saints. Little is known of his life, but he probably lived near Benares. He appears to have been a member of a low-status caste of weavers who had recently converted to Islam. Both Muslims and Hindus revere the intense and elevated devotion of his poetry, and his reputation has grown in the modern, secular era for his rejection of caste and religious prejudice. It was not unusual for such poet-saints to condemn social conventions, however, and the extent to which Kabir was personally committed to social betterment remains a matter of question. Political and economic reforms are not usually essential concerns of a poet lost in the love of God.

These translations are by India's most renowned modern poet, Nobel laureate Rabindranath Tagore, and are more polished than the vernacular preferred by Kabir.

Questions

1. What specifically Hindu and Muslim elements can you identify in these poems?
2. Would Kabir's criticism of Brahmans, caste, and other Hindu institutions be more likely to have weakened or strengthened Hinduism in this period?
3. When Kabir addresses God as "Ram," how might this differ from the use of the name in popular Hindu usage?
4. Does Kabir criticize orthodox Islam? If so, to what extent?

Songs of Kabir

Rabindranath Tagore, trans., *Songs of Kabir*
(New York: Macmillan, 1915),
pp. 45–46, 56–57, 70–71, 75–76, 80–81, 112, 142–143

If God be within the mosque, then to whom does this world belong?
If Ram be within the image which you find upon your pilgrimage, then who is there to know what happens without?
Hari is in the East: Allah is in the West. Look within your heart, for there you will find both Karim and Ram;
All men and women of the world are His living forms.
Kabir is the child of Allah and of Ram: He is my Guru, He is my Pir.[1]

[1] A Guru is a Hindu spiritual teacher; a Pir is the Sufi (Muslim) equivalent.

The Lord is in me, the Lord is in you, as life is in every seed. O servant! put false pride away, and seek for Him within you.
A million suns are ablaze with light,
The sea of blue spreads in the sky,
The fever of life is stilled, and all stains are washed away; when I sit in the midst of that world.
Hark to the unstruck bells and drums! Take your delight in love!
Rains pour down without water, and the rivers are streams of light.
One Love it is that pervades the whole world, few there are who know it fully:
They are blind who hope to see it by the light of reason, that reason which is the cause of separation—The House of Reason is very far away!
How blessed is Kabir, that amidst this great joy he sings within his own vessel.
It is the music of the meeting of soul with soul; it is the music of the forgetting of sorrows;
It is the music that transcends all coming in and all going forth.

It is the mercy of my true Guru that has made me to know the unknown;
I have learned from Him how to walk without feet, to see without eyes, to hear without ears, to drink without mouth, to fly without wings;
I have brought my love and my meditation into the land where there is no sun and moon, nor day and night.
Without eating, I have tasted of the sweetness of nectar; and without water, I have quenched my thirst.
Where there is the response of delight, there is the fullness of joy. Before whom can that joy be uttered?
Kabir says: "The Guru is great beyond words, and great is the good fortune of the disciple."

Dance, my heart! dance to-day with joy.
The strains of love fill the days and the nights with music, and the world is listening to its melodies:
Mad with joy, life and death dance to the rhythm of this music. The hills and the sea and the earth dance. The world of man dances in laughter and tears.

Why put on the robe of the monk, and live aloof from the world in lonely pride?
Behold! my heart dances in the delight of a hundred arts; and the Creator is well pleased.

O Lord Increate, who will serve Thee?
Every votary offers his worship to the God of his own creation: each day he receives service—
None seek Him, the Perfect: Brahma, the Indivisible Lord.
They believe in ten Avatars; but no Avatar can be the Infinite Spirit, for he suffers the results of his deeds:
The Supreme One must be other than this.
The Yogi, the Sanyasi, the Ascetics, are disputing one with another:
Kabir says, "O brother! he who has seen that radiance of love, he is saved."

Lamps burn in every house, O blind one! and you cannot see them.
One day your eyes shall suddenly be opened, and you shall see: and the fetters of death will fall from you.
There is nothing to say or to hear, there is nothing to do: it is he who is living, yet dead, who shall never die again.
Because he lives in solitude, therefore the Yogi says that his home is far away.
Your Lord is near: yet you are climbing the palm-tree to seek Him.
The Brahman priest goes from house to house and initiates people into faith:
Alas! the true fountain of life is beside you, and you have set up a stone to worship.
Kabir says: "I may never express how sweet my Lord is. Yoga and the telling of beads, virtue and vice—these are naught to Him."

O servant, where dost thou seek Me?
Lo! I am beside thee.
I am neither in temple nor in mosque: I am neither in Kaaba nor in Kailash:[2]

---

[2] i.e., in Mecca or Mt. Kailash, the holiest places in Islam and Hinduism, respectively.

Neither am I in rites and ceremonies, nor in Yoga and renunciation.
If thou art a true seeker, thou shalt at once see me: thou shalt meet Me in a moment of time.
Kabir says, "O Sadhu! God is the breath of all breath."

It is needless to ask of a saint the caste to which he belongs; for the priest, the warrior, the tradesman, and all the thirty-six castes, alike are seeking for God.
It is but folly to ask what the caste of a saint may be;
The barber has sought God, the washerwoman, and the carpenter—
Even Raidas was a seeker after God.
The Rishi Swapacha was a tanner by caste.[3]
Hindus and Moslems alike have achieved that End, where remains no mark of distinction.

[3] Raidas was a fifteenth century mystic of the low-status Chamar caste. Swapacha is a name often given to men of lower castes; here to one who composed Vedic hymns.

✧ Sacred Writings of the Sikhs ✧

Guru Nanak (1469–1539), the founder of the Sikh religion, was reared as a Hindu in a small village in the Punjab, where Hindu and Muslim attitudes and ways of life had mixed over the years. Nanak was a contemporary of Babur (1483–1530), the founder of the Mughal Empire, and his life thus spanned the end of the Delhi Sultanate and the years during which the Mughals were extending their power across northern India. At the same time, the West had reached the shores of India (1498), and Portuguese trading stations along the coast were soon bringing Western trading goods and Christian ideology to the land. Persian Sufi mysticism was growing stronger in the region, and the popularity of the Hindu adoration of Vishnu as a loving and earth-dwelling god continued to spread northward. In many ways, a number of disparate beliefs were beginning to coalesce in north India. Hinduism, Sufism, and Christianity were all preaching faiths in which an all-powerful god yet bound himself to humanity in love and in which the return of that love could bring the worshipper ecstatic joy. All envisioned an ethical god, who took pleasure in the good deeds of his worshippers and who was himself the greatest good. Finally, all believed that their god, or rather his personification, dwelled at times among human beings to aid, teach, and share the sorrows of being merely human. Many Indians saw these similarities and pondered whether all these formulations were simply different expressions of the same ultimate reality. Nanak was one of these.

For some time after 1500, he was employed by the governor of Punjab, but experienced revelations that called him to the preaching of his beliefs. He traveled widely in this pursuit and, according to legend, visited Mecca, Tibet, and Sri Lanka as well as much of India. For the last fifteen years of his life (1524–1539), he lived in a small village above Lahore.

Nanak's teachings resembled those of Kabir (c. 1440–1518) in many ways, being inspired by the same sources. There are enough similarities between the works of the two that Nanak is sometimes considered a disciple of Kabir. Both combined the devotionalism of the worshippers of Vishnu with the religious and social iconoclasm of the holy men of the time. They both rejected conventional forms of worship, condemned the caste system, and used the vernacular of the common people (Punjabi in the case of Nanak) rather than the classical Sanskrit or Persian of scholars and court officials. There are distinct differences, however, such as the greater consistency of Nanak's teachings and his emphasis on a fellowship of believers that would transcend divisions of race, religion, caste, lineage, and sex. Similar concepts are found later in Tulsidas (1543–1623).

Nanak's followers took the name Sikh, or disciple. According to Sikh doctrine, the divine spirit that inspired Nanak, revealing divine wisdom and ethical principles through him, continued to dwell on earth in the persons of ten successive gurus, or "preceptors." These gurus not only were the religious leaders of the faith, but also governed the community of believers. The third guru began collecting the authentic versions of Nanak's hymns that had survived and added these—974 in all—to some hymns and aphorisms by Kabir. Still others were added by the fifth guru, Arjan (1581–1606), and the whole collection, known as the Adi Granth, from which the poems included here are taken, began to assume the function of sacred scriptures among the Sikhs.

By the early seventeenth century Sikhism was losing its original eclectic inspiration and missionary fervor and was beginning to assume some of the characteristics of a closed sect. This was partially due to the conservative Muslim reaction that had followed the death of the tolerant, heterodox emperor Akbar in 1605. Rights were wrested from the Hindus, temples were closed, and many of the eclectic faiths faced persecution, which further closed Sikh society to outside influences. By the end of the seventeenth century the Sikhs had evolved into a militant community, suspicious of outsiders, and with a distinctive appearance and communal cohesion in the region of the Punjab. Sikhism, originally conceived by Nanak as a unifying association that would transcend caste distinctions by the power of common beliefs, became itself an exclusive community. The decline of the Mughal Empire and threats by Afghan and Persian invaders in the eighteenth century accentuated the political independence, militancy, and anti-Muslim sentiment of the Sikhs.

Two well-illustrated websites on Sikhism are http://www.sikh-heritage.co.uk and http://www.sikh-history.com.

Questions

1. What are the similarities and differences between Kabir and Guru Nanak?
2. What does Guru Nanak seem to think is the role of women?
3. Are there any indications that these ideas would become the basis of a religious sect? of a militant community?

Sacred Writing of the Sikhs

Jodh Singh, Kapur Singh, Bawa Harkishen Singh, and Khushwant Singh, trans., *Sacred Writings of the Sikhs,* UNESCO Collection of Representative Works, Indian Series (London: Unwin Hyman, 1960)

There is one God,
Eternal Truth is His Name;
Maker of all things,
Fearing nothing and at enmity with nothing,
Timeless is His Image;
Not begotten, being of His own Being:
By the grace of the Guru, made known to men.
Jap: The Meditation

As He was in the beginning: The Truth,
So throughout the ages,
He ever has been: The Truth,
So even now He is Truth Immanent,
So for ever and ever he shall be Truth Eternal.

There is no counting of men's prayers,
There is no counting their ways of adoration.
Thy lovers, O Lord, are numberless;
Numberless those who read aloud from the Vedas;
Numberless those Yogis who are detached from the world;

Numberless are Thy Saints contemplating,
Thy virtues and Thy wisdom;
Numberless are the benevolent, the lovers of their kind.
Numberless Thy heroes and martyrs
Facing the steel of their enemies;
Numberless those who in silence
Fix their deepest thoughts upon Thee;

How can an insignificant creature like myself
Express the vastness and wonder of Thy creation?
I am too petty to have anything to offer Thee;
I cannot, even once, be a sacrifice unto Thee.
To abide by Thy Will, O Lord, is man's best offering;
Thou who art Eternal, abiding in Thy Peace.

There is no counting fools, the morally blind;
No counting thieves and the crooked,
No counting the shedders of the innocent blood;
No counting the sinners who go on sinning;

No counting the liars who take pleasure in lies;
No counting the dirty wretches who live on filth;
No counting the calumniators
Who carry about on their heads their loads of sin.

Thus saith Nanak, lowliest of the lowly:
I am too petty to have anything to offer Thee;
I cannot, even once, be a sacrifice unto Thee.
To abide by Thy Will, O Lord, is man's best offering;
Thou who art Eternal, abiding in Thy Peace.

Countless are Thy Names, countless Thine abodes;
Completely beyond the grasp of the imagination
Are Thy myriad realms;
Even to call them myriad is foolish.

Yet through words and through letters
Is Thy Name uttered and Thy praise expressed;
In words we praise Thee,
In words we sing of Thy virtues.

It is in the words that we write and speak about Thee,
In words on man's forehead
Is written man's destiny,
But God who writes that destiny
Is free from the bondage of words.

As God ordaineth, so man receiveth.
All creation is His Word made manifest;
Except in the Light of His Word
There is no way.

How can an insignificant creature like myself
Express the vastness and wonder of Thy creation?
I am too petty to have anything to offer Thee;
I cannot, even once, be a sacrifice unto Thee.
To abide by Thy Will, O Lord, is man's best offering;
Thou who art Eternal, abiding in Thy Peace.

Let compassion be thy mosque,
Let faith be thy prayer mat,
Let honest living be thy Koran,
Let modesty be the rules of observance,
Let piety be the fasts thou keepest;
In such wise strive to become a Moslem:
Right conduct the Ka'ba; Truth the Prophet,
Good deeds thy prayer;
Submission to the Lord's Will thy rosary;
Nanak, if this thou do, the Lord will be thy Protector.

Of a woman are we conceived,
Of a woman we are born,
To a woman are we betrothed and married,
It is a woman who is friend and partner of life,
It is woman who keeps the race going,
Another companion is sought when the life-partner dies,
Through woman are established social ties,
Why should we consider woman cursed and condemned

When from woman are born leaders and rulers.
From woman alone is born a woman,
Without woman there can be no human birth.
Without woman, O Nanak, only the True One exists.
Be it men or be it women,
Only those who sing His glory
Are blessed and radiant with His Beauty,
In His Presence and with His grace
They appear with a radiant face.

A true Ksatriya, of the warrior caste, is one whose valour
Shows itself in every detail of his life.
The aim of life is loving kindness,
Which he gives to the deserving,
And so becomes acceptable to God.
Any man who moved by greed, preaches falsehood,
In the end must pay the penalty for his deeds.

When the hands, feet and other parts
Of the body are besmeared with filth,
They are cleansed with water;
When a garment is defiled
It is rinsed with soapsuds;
So when the mind is polluted with sin,
We must scrub it in love of the Name.
We do not become sinners or saints,
By merely saying we are;
It is actions that are recorded;
According to the seed we sow, is the fruit we reap.
By God's Will, O Nanak,
Man must either be saved or endure new births.

On hearing of the Lord,
All men speak of His greatness;
Only he that hath seen Him
Can know how great is He.
Who can conceive of His worth
Or who can describe Him?
Those who seek to describe Thee
Are lost in Thy depths.

O Great Lord, of depth unfathomable,
Ocean of virtues!
Who knoweth the bounds of Thy shores?
All the contemplatives
Have met and sought to contemplate Thee;
All the weighers of worth
Have met and sought to weigh Thy worth;
All the theologians and the mystics,
All the preachers and their teachers
Have not been able to grasp
One jot of Thy greatness.

All truths, all fervent austerities, every excellent act,
Every sublime achievement of the adepts,
Are Thy gifts, O Lord: without Thee
No man could attain perfection;
But where Thou hast granted Thy grace to a man,
Nothing can stand in his way.

How vain are the words of those that seek to praise Thee,
Thy treasuries are already filled with Thy praises;
He to whom Thou givest freely,
What should he do but praise Thee?

Saith Nanak: The True One is He
From whom all perfection springs.

✧ Akbar Nama ✧

Abu-l Fazl

The Mughal Empire (1526–1858) was the sixth Muslim dynasty to rule in India. During the last century of its reign it was sustained by the British, who utilized the Mughal emperors as figureheads for their own increasing authority in the land. The Muslim Mughals left a heritage of art, architecture, literature, and law that continues to influence India today. The British in India modeled their administration after that of the Mughals, even to the point of continuing Court Persian as the language of record-keeping. For the first 100 years they ruled India, the British claimed to be no more than subjects of the Mughal emperors, governing in their name.

The greatest ruler of this empire was Akbar (r. 1556–1605), grandson of the empire's founder, whose conquests and administrative reforms did much to establish Mughal power on solid ground and gain for it a century of ascendancy in north India. The greater part of Akbar's reign was spent planning and executing military campaigns. He was a heroic commander who personally led the attacks on his strongest enemies, although he preferred to negotiate a surrender rather than fight. He married Rajput princesses in order to win over their Hindu kinsmen and overcame the reluctance of Hindus to intermarry with Muslims by treating his new kinsmen as imperial nobility.

Although proclaiming himself a true Muslim, Akbar displayed other signs of an individualistic approach to a religion that others followed with a conservative fervor. In 1579 Akbar invited Jesuit scholars to his court and appointed one of them as tutor to his son Murad. His deference toward his Christian visitors aroused the suspicions of many of his coreligionists. These suspicions grew even deeper when Akbar issued a decree declaring himself a *mujtahid* (infallible authority) in religious affairs, an act of presumption that outraged orthodox Muslims and led to a short-lived rebellion. He then attempted to establish a new, eclectic "Divine Faith," designed to join all in a single worship, but gained little support for such a radical innovation.

Akbar's religious policies have attracted a good deal of attention over the years. He has been described alternately as a liberal Muslim who was very tolerant of other religions or as a man who combined Indian ideas of divine kingship with Muslim Sufic mysticism. Some Pakistani scholars have argued that he was a heretic who tried to suppress Islamic orthodoxy.

Akbar's religious policy was one of the great strengths of his administration. Christian traders favored him in the secret hope that he could be won over to their faith. His tolerance of Hinduism and his admission of Hindus to the ranks of his administration gained the empire valuable support, secured it a peaceful and relatively friendly subject population, and gained Akbar allies against ultraorthodox Muslims who might have attempted to drive him into a holy war against the idolatrous Hindus, which would have destroyed the prosperity of the land and thus weakened the empire he was attempting to build. Akbar held that the emperor was the sovereign of all his people and should act in the interests of all. He implemented reforms that benefited his Hindu subjects, such as the abolition of the Muslim-imposed pilgrim tax, and he encouraged interaction among religious groups in the hope of instilling greater mutual understanding among his heterogeneous people.

It was this enlightened approach to religious matters that gained him permanent fame in the verses of the *Akbar Nama*. The author, Shaikh Abu-l Fazl 'Allami (1551–1602), had come to the Mughal court, where his elder brother Faizi was court poet, in 1568. As the leaders of radical religious thought at the court, the brothers were condemned as heretics by conservative Muslims there. Finding in Akbar a kindred spirit, Abu-l Fazl was soon converted from Akbar's servant and sycophant into his true friend and admirer. For this reason, the *Akbar Nama* is more than the simple glorification of a ruler—it is a song of sincere appreciation. Seeing in Akbar both an emperor and a friend, Abu-l Fazl and his brother supported and encouraged him in the tolerance and religious radicalism he seemed to be pursuing. In the end, however, neither the emperor Akbar nor the poet Abu-l Fazl could contain the forces of distrust and intolerance among the Indian people.

Like Mohandas Gandhi centuries later, Akbar's dream of a united India was thwarted by the twin forces of prejudice and fanaticism. Conservative Muslim elements joined in opposition to him, and rebellion broke out. Prince Salim, son of Akbar and a rebel leader, captured the poet Abu-l Fazl in 1602 and had him put to death. With Akbar's death in 1605, Prince Salim assumed the title Emperor Jahangir (r. 1605–1627). An imperial policy of increasing intolerance of non-Muslims emerged over the years, and the Mughal Empire steadily lost the support of the mass of the population of India. The vision of Akbar and Abu-l Fazl of a land of unity and tolerance had clearly come before its time.

Akbar was a great patron of the arts and many museums have good collections. One example is the Metropolitan Museum of Art in New York City: http://www.metmuseum.org.

Questions

1. What qualities does Abu-l Fazl praise in Akbar?
2. What faults does Akbar find in the Islamic theologians?
3. Does Akbar reject Islam?
4. Does Akbar's concept of "truth" embrace all pure expressions of the ultimate reality, or does it construct a new exclusive truth?

Akbar Nama

Abu-l Fazl, *Akbar Nama*, trans., Henry Beveridge (Calcutta: Royal Asiatic Society, 1897), pp. 364–367, 369–372

Although God-given wisdom and the science of Divine knowledge (theology) adorn his holy personality and illumine his actions, yet, owing to the utter marvelousness of his nature, he every now and then draws a special veil over his countenance, and exercises world-sway and speaks and acts in accordance with the requirements of the time. At the present day, when the morning-breeze of fortune is blowing, and the star of success is continually acquiring fresh radiance, he, by his practical knowledge and farsightedness, makes external ability the veil of spirituality and appraises the value of the mortifiers of the passions, and the calibre of scientists. It has been mentioned that he, in his ample search after truth, had laid the foundation of a noble seat for intellectual meetings. His sole and sublime idea was that, as in the external administration of the dominion, which is conjoined with eternity, the merits of the knowers of the things of this world had by profundity of vision, and observance of justice, been made conspicuous, and there had ceased to be a brisk market for pretence and favouritism, so might the masters of science and ethics, and the devotees of piety and contemplation, be tested, the principles of faiths and creeds be examined, religions be investigated, the proofs and evidences for each be considered, and the pure gold and the alloy be separated from evil commixture. In a short space of time a beautiful, detached building was erected, and the fraudulent vendors of impostures put to sleep in the privy chamber of contempt. A noble palace was provided for the spiritual world, and the pillars of Divine knowledge rose high. At this time, when the center of the Caliphate (Fatepur Sikri) was glorified by H.M. [His Majesty]'s advent, the former institutions were renewed, and the temple of Divine knowledge was on Thursday nights illuminated by the light of the holy mind. On 20 Mihr, Divine month, 3 October 1578, and in that house of worship, the lamp of the privy chamber of detachment was kindled in the banqueting-hall of social life. The coin of the hivers of wisdom in colleges and cells was brought to the test. The clear wine was separated from the lees, and good coin from the adulterated. The wide capacity and the toleration of the Shadow of God were unveiled. Sufi, philosopher, orator, jurist, Sunni, Shia, Brahman, Jati, Siura Carbak, Nazarene, Jew, Sabi (Sabian), Zoroastrian, and others enjoyed exquisite pleasure by beholding the calmness of the assembly, the sitting of the world-lord in the lofty pulpit (*mimbar*), and the adornment of the pleasant abode of impartiality. The treasures of secrets were opened out without fear of hostile seekers after battle. The just and truth-perceiving ones of each sect emerged from haughtiness and conceit, and began their search anew. They displayed profundity and meditation, and gathered eternal bliss on the divan of greatness. The conceited and quarrelsome from evilness of disposition and shortness of thought descended into the mire of presumption and sought their profit in loss. Being guided by ignorant companions, and from the predominance of a somnolent fortune, they went into disgrace. The conferences were excellently arranged by the acuteness and keen quest of truth of the world's Khedive. Every time, eye and heart gained fresh lustre, and the lamp of vigils acquired new. The candle of investigation was lighted for those who loved darkness and sequacity. The families of the colleges and monasteries were tested. The handle of wealth and the material of sufficiency came into the grasp of the needy occupants of the summit of expectation. The fame of this faith-adorning method of world-bestowing made home bitter to inquirers and caused them to love exile. The Shahinshah's court became the home of the inquirers of the seven climes, and the assemblage of the wise of every religion and sect. The veneer and the counterfeitness of all those who by feline tricks and stratagems had come forth in the garb of wisdom were revealed. A few irreverent and crafty spirits continued their old tactics after the appearance of Truth and its concomitant convictions, and indulged in brawling. Their idea was that as in the great assemblies of former rulers the purpose of science and the designs of wisdom had been but little explored owing to the crowd of men, the inattention of the governor of the feast, the briskness of the market of praters, etc., so perhaps in this august assemblage they might succeed by the length of their tongues, and a veil might be hung over the occiput (*fararu*) of truth. The Khedive of wisdom by the glory of his mind carried out the work to a conclusion deliberately and impartially, and in this praiseworthy fashion, which is seldom found in the saints of asceticism—how then is it to be found in world rulers?—tested the various coins of mortals. Many men became stained with shame and chose loss of fame, while some acquired wisdom and emerged from the hollow of obscurity to eminence. Reason was exalted, and the star of fortune shone for the acquirers of knowledge. The bigoted 'Ulama and the routine-lawyers, who reckoned themselves among the chiefs of philosophies and leaders of enlightenment, found their position difficult. The veil was removed from the face of many of them. The house of evil-thinking coiners became the abode of a thousand suspicions and slanders. Though the wicked and crooked-minded and disaffected were always speaking foolishly about the pious Khedive, yet at this time they had a new foundation for their calumnies, and descended into the pit of eternal ruin. Inasmuch as the warmth of the Shahinshah's graciousness increases daily, and he was aware of the ignorance of those turbulent ones, he did not proceed against them with physical and spiritual vigour and with external and internal majesty. Rather, he restrained his heart and tongue from uttering his disgust, and did not allow the dust of chagrin to settle on the skirt of his soul. In a short space of time many of these fortunately fell into fatal evils and suffered losses and died, while some who were of a good sort became ashamed, and took up the work (of study) anew. From a long time it was the custom that the dull and superficial regarded the heartfelt words of holy souls as foolishness. They recognized wisdom nowhere but in the schools, and did not know that acquired knowledge is for the most part stained with doubts and suspicions. Insight is that which without schooling illuminates the pure temple of the heart. The inner soul receives rays from holy heaven. From eternity, the ocean of Divine bounties has been in motion, and the cup of those who are worthy of the world of creation is filled to the brim therefrom. Always have the magnates of Use and Wont in spite of their great knowledge sought the explanation of wisdom and ethics (*'ilm it 'aural*) from this company of the pure in heart, and have waited in the ante-chamber of the simple and beautiful of soul, and have gathered bliss therefrom. Accordingly histories tell of this, and its transpires in biographies (?). God be praised for that at this day the Lord of Lords of inspired (*laduni*) wisdom is represented by the Holy Personality of the Shahinshah. The difficulties of sect upon sect of mankind are made easy by the flashings of his sacred soul. The attainment of enlightenment is not the first robe of honour which the eternal needle sews. He who knows the secrets of the past, and the reader of ancient stories, is well aware of this. Still more is it known to the awakened, the truth-choosing and the acute! May the Almighty God ever keep verdant and watered this tree which is rich in spiritual and material fruit!

One night, the assembly in the 'Ibadatkhana was increasing the light of truth. Padre Radif, one of the Nazarene sages, who was singular for his understanding and ability, was making points in that feast of intelligence. Some of the untruthful bigots came forward in a blundering way to answer him. Owing to the calmness of the august assembly, and the increasing light of justice, it became clear that each of these was weaving a circle of old acquisitions, and was not following the highway of proof, and that the explanation of the riddle of truth was not present to their thoughts. The veil was nearly being stripped, once for all, from their procedure. They were ashamed, and abandoned such discourse, and applied themselves to perverting the words of the Gospels. But they could not silence their antagonist by such arguments. The Padre quietly and with an air of conviction said, "Alas, that such things should be thought to be true! In fact, if this faction have such an opinion of our Book, and regard the Furqan (the Quran) as the pure word of God, it is proper that a heaped fire be lighted. We shall take the Gospels in our hands, and the Ulama of that faith shall take their book, and then let us enter that testing-place of truth. The escape of any one will be a sign of his truthfulness." The liverless and black-hearted fellows wavered, and in reply to the challenge had recourse to bigotry and wrangling. This cowardice and effrontery displeased his (Akbar's) equitable soul, and the banquet of enlightenment was made resplendent by acute observations. Continually, in those day-like nights, glorious subtleties and profound words dropped from his pearl-filled mouth. Among them was this: "Most persons, from intimacy with those who adorn their outside, but are inwardly bad, think that outward semblance, and the letter of Muhammadanism, profit without internal conviction. Hence we by fear and force compelled many believers in the Brahman (i.e., Hindu) religion to adopt the faith of our ancestors. Now that the light of truth has taken possession of our soul, it has become clear that in this distressful place of contrarities (the world), where darkness of comprehension and conceit are heaped up, fold upon fold, a single step cannot be taken without the torch of proof, and that that creed is profitable which is adopted with the approval of wisdom. To repeat the creed, to remove a piece of skin (i.e., to become circumcised) and to place the end of one's bones on the ground (i.e., the head in adoration) from dread of the Sultan, is not seeking after God."

Verse.
Obedience is not the placing of your forehead in the dust.
Produce truth, for sincerity is not situated in the forehead.

The first step in this perilous desert is with a high courage, and an exalted determination to rise up and do battle with the protean and presumptuous carnal soul, and by rigorous self examination to make Anger and Lust the subjects of Sultan Reason, and to erase from the heart the marks of censurable sentiments. Mayhap the Sun of Proof will emerge from behind the veil of Error and make one a truth-worshipper, and afterward he may by secret attraction draw to himself one of the inquirers after the Path. Such load-stones are produced from the mine of asceticism (*riyazat*). Or it may be that by virtue of talisman and the might of fascination he may bring him into his circle. Should the latter go astray and fall into the pit of not doing God's will, yet shall he not be stained with the dust of blame. He also said, "We blame ourselves for what we did in accordance with old rules and before the truth about faith had shed its rays on our heart." The fortunate and auspicious, on hearing these enlightening words, hastened to the abode of the light of search and set themselves to amend their ways, while the somnolent and perverse were full of disturbance. Inasmuch as the fierce winds of indiscrimination had laid hold of the four corners of the world, he mentioned the rules of various religions, and described their various excellencies. The acute sovereign gave no weight to common talk, and praised whatever was good in any religion. He often adorned the tablet of his tongue by saying "He is a man who makes Justice the guide of the path of inquiry, and takes from every sect what is consonant to reason. Perhaps in this way the lock, whose key has been lost, may be opened." In this connexion, he praised the truth-seeking of the natives of India, and eloquently described the companionship of the men of that country in the day of disaster, and how they played away for the sake of Fidelity (lit. in the shadow of), Property, Life, Reputation, and Religion, which are reckoned as comprising the four goods of the world's market. He also dwelt upon the wonderful way in which the women of that country become ashes whenever the day of calamity arrives. This bliss-collecting class has several divisions. Some protagonists of the path of righteousness yield up their lives merely on hearing of the inevitable lot of their husbands. Many sensualists of old times were, from ignorance and irreflection, unable to read such exquisite creatures by the lines of the forehead, or the record of their behavior, and entered with loss the ravine of experiment, and cast away recklessly the priceless jewel! Some deliberately and with open brow enter the flames along with their husband's corpse, or with some token of him who hath gone to the land of annihilation.

Some whom sacrifice of life and fellowship do not make happy, yet, from fear of men's reproach, observe the letter of love, and descend into the mouth of the fire. He said to the learned Christians, "Since you reckon the reverencing of women as part of your religion, and allow not more than one wife to a man, it would not be wonderful if such fidelity and life-sacrifice were found among your women. The extraordinary thing is that it occurs among those of the Brahman (i.e., the Hindu) religion. There are numerous concubines, and many of them are neglected and unappreciated and spend their days unfructuously in the privy chamber of chastity, yet in spite of such bitterness of life they are flaming torches of love and fellowship." On hearing such noble recitals those present remained silent in the hall of reply, and their tongues reddened with surprise. The Divine message filled with joy all the seekers after wisdom in the august assemblage.

✧ Hanuman Chalisa ✧

Hanuman has become one of the most beloved deities in the Hindu pantheon, revered by nearly every Hindu sect. There are probably more temples devoted to Hanuman than to any other deity in India, and recitation of the *Hanuman Chalisa*, given here in its entirely, is one of the most common religious practices.

There may have been precursors of Hanuman in the Vedas, but the major early source is the epic poem *Ramayana* by Valmiki, composed from oral traditions. It was originally passed down orally before it was preserved in written Sanskrit sometime before the third century CE. It is more beloved than the other great Sanskrit epic, the older and longer *Mahabharata*, and it is more influential in art and literature.

The *Ramayana* is the story of Rama, a prince who was exiled for fourteen years because his stepmother wanted her son Bharata to succeed to the throne. Bharata offered to renounce the throne, but Rama yielded to their parents' wishes. His faithful wife Sita and his brother Lakshman joined him in his forest retreat. Later Ravana, the evil King of Lanka (now considered to be present-day Sri Lanka), fell in love with Sita and abducted her. Rama enlisted the aid of a monkey army, with Hanuman at their head, to build a causeway across to Lanka.

They defeated Ravana with the aid of Hanuman's superpowers, released Sita, and brought her safely back to Ayodhya. Hanuman is credited with leaping to the island, finding Sita, escaping captivity, burning Lanka, and saving Lakshman's life by flying to the Himalayas and bringing back an entire mountain that contained a magic healing herb.

There are numerous versions of the epic throughout India and

Southeast Asia. The most significant for the story of Hanuman is the *Ramacharitamanasa* by the north Indian poet Tulsidas (1543–1623). It was composed not in Sanskrit, but in a Hindi dialect, which made it accessible to many more people. By this time, the dominant form of Hindu worship was devotionalism (*bhakti*). Rama was transformed from a heroic prince with godlike qualities into a full-fledged divinity, the seventh incarnation (avatar) of the god Vishnu. By the time of Kabir, the name *Rama* had come to designate the Supreme Being. The *Ramacharitamanasa* stresses devotion to God through Rama, and Hanuman is portrayed as the ultimate devotee of Rama. His superpowers are a product of his devotion.

Folk tales appear to have increasingly emphasized Hanuman's divinity. He was considered the descendant of deities and an avatar of Shiva. His courage, strength, wisdom, abilities, and celibacy, as well as his devotion to Rama, convinced devotees that he could confer power (*shakti*) on them. The *Hanuman Chalisa* summarizes these tales, along with the many names by which he was known.

Devotees believe that the *Hanuman Chalisa* was also written by Tulsidas, whom they consider to have been divinely inspired. In fact, it is a much later work, probably composed in the late eighteenth or early nineteenth century.

Many images of Hanuman are posted on the Internet. Examples are at http://hanumaanchalisa.tripod.com.

Questions

1. What powers does Hanuman have that confer benefits on people who worship him?
2. Why do you think the *Hanuman Chalisa* repeatedly associates Hanuman with Shiva, Vishnu (Rama), and other Hindu deities? Does this practice elevate him from the hero of a folk tale and local deity to an authentic member of the pantheon himself?
3. To what extent are the points emphasized in the *Hanuman Chalisa* a continuation of the *bhakti* tradition?

✧ ✧ ✧ ✧ ✧

Hanuman Chalisa

“Appendix. Two Poems in Praise of Hanuman (Attributed to Tulsidas),” in Philip Lutgendorf, *Hanuman’s Tale: The Messages of a Divine Monkey* (Oxford: Oxford University Press, 2007), pp. 397–399

Hanumān Cālīsā (Forty Verses to Hanuman)
(invocatory couplets)
Having polished, with the dust of my master’s feet, the mirror of my heart,
I narrate the pure fame of Raghupati, which bestows life’s four fruits.
Knowing this body to be void of intelligence, I recall the Son of the Wind.
Grant me strength, intelligence, wisdom, and remove my afflictions and shortcomings.
(*verses*)
1. Victory to Hanuman, ocean of wisdom and virtue,
Hail monkey lord, illuminator of the three worlds.
2. Rama’s emissary, abode of matchless power,
Anjani’s son, named “Son of the Wind.”
3. Great hero, mighty as a thunderbolt,
remover of bad thoughts and companion to good.
4. Golden-hued and splendidly adorned,
with heavy earrings and curly locks.
5. In your hands shine mace and banner,
a thread of munja grass adorns your shoulder.
6. Shiva’s son and Kesari’s joy,
your glory is sung throughout the world.
7. Supremely wise, virtuous, and clever,
you are ever intent on Rama’s tasks.
8. You relish hearing the Lord’s deeds,
Rama, Lakshmana, and Sita dwell in your heart.
9. Taking tiny form you showed yourself to Sita,
assuming awesome form you burned Lanka.
10. Taking terrible form you slew demons
and completed Ramachandra’s mission.
11. Bringing the healing herb, you revived Lakshmana,
and Rama, overjoyed, clasped you to his breast.
12. Greatly did the Raghu Lord praise you:
“Brother, you’re as dear to me as Bharat!

13. May the thousand-mouthed serpent sing your fame!"
So saying, Shri's Lord held you in his embrace.
14. Sanaka and the sages, Brahma and the gods,
great saints, Narada, Sarasvati, and the king of snakes,
15. Yama, Kubera, and the directional guardians,
poets, and pandits—none can express your glory.
16. You rendered great service to Sugriva,
presented him to Rama, and gave him kingship.
17. Vibhishana heeded your counsel
and became Lord of Lanka, as the whole world knows.
18. The sun is two thousand leagues away,
yet you swallowed it, thinking it a sweet fruit.
19. With the Lord's ring in your mouth,
you leapt the sea—what wonder in that?
20. Every arduous task in this world
becomes easy by your grace.
21. You are the guardian of Rama's door,
none enters without your leave.
22. Sheltered by you, one gains all delight,
protected by you, one fears no one.
23. You alone can contain your glory,
the three worlds tremble at your roar.
24. Ghosts and spirits cannot come near,
Great Hero, when your name is uttered.
25. Disease is destroyed and all pain removed,
brave Hanuman, by constantly repeating your name.
26. Hanuman releases from affliction
those who focus on him in thought, word, and deed.
27. Rama the renunciant reigns above all,
you carry out all his work.
28. Whoever brings any yearning to you
obtains the fruit of immortal life.
29. Your splendor fills the four ages,
your fame shines throughout the world.
30. You are the guardian of saints and sages,
the destroyer of demons, the darling of Rama.
31. You grant the eight powers and nine treasures,
such was the boon given by Mother Janaki.
32. You possess the elixir of Rama
and remain eternally his servant.
33. Singing your praise, one finds Rama
and forgets the sorrows of countless lives.

34. At death, one goes to Rama's realm
or is born on earth as his devotee.
35. Pay no heed to any other deity,
serving Hanuman, one obtains all delight.
36. All affliction ceases, all pain is erased,
when one recalls the mighty hero, Hanuman.
37. Victory, victory, victory to Lord Hanuman!
Be merciful even as is the Master.
38. Whoever recites this a hundred times
is released from bondage and gains bliss.
39. One who reads this Hanuman Chalisa
gains success—Gauri's Lord is witness.
40. Says Tulsidas, Hari's constant servant,
"Lord, make your abode in my heart."
(*benedictory couplet*)
Son of the Wind, banisher of affliction, embodiment of auspiciousness,
dwell in my heart, King of Gods, together with Rama, Lakshmana, and Sita.

✧ On the Burning of Widows ✧

Ram Mohan Roy

The English East India Company had been trading in the Indian subcontinent since 1600. Along with French and Dutch traders, it broke the monopoly of Europe's trade with India enjoyed by the Portuguese since 1500. During the Seven Years' War (1756–1763), Company forces defeated their competitors and established British commercial supremacy in the region. For the next century, this commercial corporation acted increasingly as an independent government in India, administering all British affairs there, annexing territory, forming its own army and navy, and establishing protectorates over native princes.

Company administration was limited primarily to the maintenance of law and order, revenue collection, and bureaucratic efficiency. In the first half of the nineteenth century, however, the Company was forced to expand its role in other areas. Parliament coerced the Company to admit missionaries after 1813 and required it to develop a policy for the education of Indians in European-style schools. Some of the British in India had developed a high regard for Indian literature and philosophy. Company officials founded the Royal Asiatic Society in 1784 and promoted scholarly research into the history and civilization of India; it was a Company employee who first recognized the relationship between Sanskrit and the Western European languages. Still others advocated providing Indians with a thoroughly British education, for both philosophical and practical reasons, the latter including gaining the Company a cheap and steady supply of well-trained, subordinate employees. A few missionaries urged that Western-style education be provided in the native spoken languages or "vernaculars" of India.

The debate was settled by a resolution in 1835: the Company would train an elite group of Indians in Western subjects, and the instruction would be in English. By this time, a small stratum of English-educated Indians had come into being, and Ram Mohan Roy (1774–1833) was outstanding among these.

Bengal and especially Calcutta had the most intensive contact with the British, and both areas had become cosmopolitan, bustling commercial centers. Generous land-revenue settlements put large amounts of money in the hands of Bengali *zamindars* (landholders), many of whom sublet their estates to others and moved into Calcutta to swell the Indian elite concentrated there. Other members of the Bengali intelligentsia learned to live by their wits in this nontraditional society, becoming lawyers, tutors, translators, or journalists. This generation prospered from their contacts with British institutions and absorbed Western ideas. They studied both Sanskrit and Bengali literature and founded a school, Hindu College, specifically for the purpose of bringing the benefits of Western civilization, purged of its Christian content, to India.

Ram Mohan Roy stands out from other Indian intellectuals by his personal synthesis of Western and Indian ideas. He was a social and educational reformer whose works made a deep impact on Indian intellectual life. An English-educated Brahman from Bengal, he was a writer and orator who established newspapers, founded schools, and campaigned against social abuses such as infanticide, polygamy, and the ritual act of immolating a widow on her husband's funeral pyre (*sati*, literally "virtuous woman"), all of which he believed were the results of the degeneration of India's ancient traditions. Roy criticized Christian missionaries for their hostility to Indian culture and its religious ideals.

Widow-burning was infrequent, practiced only by members of certain higher castes, who believed it brought them great merit. As the British extended their territorial control, they attempted to suppress the practice. In fact, they appear to have succeeded in increasing the practice, perhaps because their opposition served to publicize and popularize the incidents that occurred. Western opposition seemed to highlight for many the Indian character of the custom. In a pamphlet published in Bengali and in English in 1818, Roy challenged that point of view by opposing the burning of widows on purely Hindu Indian grounds, drawing his arguments from Sanskrit law books. Despite his persuasive exposition, widow-burning was not outlawed in Bengal until

1829, but thereafter became rare in India. Nevertheless, it has never been completely eliminated, and cases still occur.

Questions

1. What does Roy emphasize in his autobiographical sketch? What does he omit?
2. What are the strongest arguments the Advocate makes for the practice of widow-burning? How does Roy refute these?
3. What does widow-burning imply about the status of women in Hindu India?

On the Burning of Widows

Autobiographical Sketch

Jogendra Chunder Ghose, ed., *The English Works of Raja Ram Mohan Roy*, vol. 1 (Calcutta: Srikanta Roy, 1901), pp. 123–128, 130–132, 134–138, 317–320

My DEAR FRIEND,

In conformity with the wish, you have frequently expressed, that I should give you an outline of my life, I have now the pleasure to give you the following very brief sketch.

My ancestors were Brahmans of a high order, and, from time immemorial, were devoted to the religious duties of their race, down to my fifth progenitor, who about one hundred and forty years ago gave up spiritual exercises for worldly pursuits and aggrandisement. His descendants ever since have followed his example, and, according to the usual fate of courtiers, with various success, sometimes rising to honour and sometimes falling; sometimes rich and sometimes poor; sometimes excelling in success, sometimes miserable through disappointment. But my maternal ancestors, being of the sacerdotal order by profession as well as by birth, and of a family than which none holds a higher rank in that profession, have up to the present day uniformly adhered to a life of religious observances and devotion, preferring peace and tranquility of mind to the excitements of ambition, and all the allurements of worldly grandeur.

In conformity with the usage of my paternal race, and the wish of my father, I studied the Persian and Arabic languages—these being indispensable to those who attached themselves to the courts of the Mahommedan princes; and agreeably to the usage of my maternal relations, I devoted myself to the study of the Sanscrit and the theological works written in it, which contain the body of Hindoo literature, law and religion.

When about the age of sixteen, I composed a manuscript calling in question the validity of the idolatrous system of the Hindoos. This, together with my known sentiments on that subject, having produced a coolness between me and my immediate kindred, I proceeded on my travels, and passed through different countries, chiefly within, but some beyond, the bonds of Hindoostan, with a feeling of great aversion to the establishment of the British power in India. When I had reached the age of twenty, my father recalled me, and restored me to his favour; after which I first saw and began to associate with Europeans, and soon after made myself tolerably acquainted with their laws and form of government. Finding them generally more intelligent, more steady and moderate in their conduct, I gave up my prejudice against them, and became inclined in their favour, feeling persuaded that their rule, though a foreign yoke, would lead more speedily and surely to the amelioration of the native inhabitants; and I enjoyed the confidence of several of them even in their public capacity. My continued controversies with the Brahmans on the subject of their idolatry and superstition, and my interference with their custom of burning widows, and other pernicious practices, revived and increased their animosity against me; and through their influence with my family, my father was again obliged to withdraw his countenance openly, though his limited pecuniary support was still continued to me.

After my father's death I opposed the advocates of idolatry with still greater boldness. Availing myself of the art of printing, now established in India, I published various works and pamphlets against their errors, in the native and foreign languages. This raised such a feeling against me, that I was at last deserted by every person except two or three Scotch friends, to whom, and the nation to which they belong, I always feel grateful.

The ground which I took in all my controversies was, not that of opposition to Brahmanism, but to a perversion of it; and I endeavoured to show that the idolatry of the Brahmans was contrary to the practice of their ancestors, and the principles of the ancient books and authorities which they profess to revere and obey. Notwithstanding the violence of the opposition and resistance to my opinions, several highly respectable persons, both among my own relation and others, began to adopt the same sentiments.

I now felt a strong wish to visit Europe, and obtain by personal observation, a more thorough insight into its manners, customs, religion, and political institution. I refrained, however, from carrying this intention into effect until the friends who coincided in my sentiments should be increased in number and strength. My expectations having been at length realised, in November, 1830, I embarked for England, as the discussion of the East India Company's charter was expected to come on, by which the treatment of the natives of India, and its future government, would be determined for many years to come, and an appeal to the King in Council, against the abolition of the practice of burning widows, was to be heard before the Privy Council; and his Majesty the Emperor of Delhi had likewise commissioned me to bring before the authorities in England certain encroachments on his rights by the East India Company. I accordingly arrived in England in April, 1831.

I hope you will excuse the brevity of this sketch, as I have no leisure at present to enter into particulars, and

I remain, &c.,

Rammohun Roy

Conference Between an Advocate for, and an Opponent of the Practice of Burning Widows Alive

Advocate. I am surprised that you endeavour to oppose the practice of Concremation and Postcremation of widows, as long observed in this country.

Opponent. Those who have no reliance on the Shastru [*sastras,* scriptures], and those who take delight in the self-destruction of women, may well wonder that we should oppose that suicide which is forbidden by all the Shastrus, and by every race of men.

Advocate. You have made an improper assertion in alleging that Concremation and Postcremation are forbidden by the Shastrus. I Hear what Ungira [Anguiras, a sage] and other saints have said on this subject:

"That woman who, on the death of her husband, ascends the burning pile with him, is exalted to heaven, as equal to Uroondhooti [Arundhati, wife of a sage]. (1)

"She who follows her husband to another world, shall dwell in a region of joy for so many years as there are hairs in the human body, or thirty-five millions. (2)

"As a serpent-catcher forcibly draws a snake from his hole, thus raising her husband by her power, she enjoys delight along with him. (3)

"The woman who follows her husband expiates the sins of three races; her father's line, her mother's line, and the family of him to whom she was given a virgin. (4)

"There possessing her husband as her chiefest good, herself the best of women, enjoying the highest delights, she partakes of bliss with her husband as long as fourteen Indrus [the god Indra] reign. (5)

"Even though the man had slain a Brahman, or returned evil for good, or killed an intimate friend, the woman expiates those crimes. (6)

"There is no other way known for a virtuous woman except ascending the pile of her husband. It should be understood that there is no other duty whatever after the death of her husband:" (7)

Hear also what Vyas [Vyasa, a sage] has written in the parable of the pigeon:

"A pigeon, devoted to her husband, after his death entered the flames, and ascending to heaven, she there found her husband:" (8)

And hear Hareet's [Harita, a sage] words:

"As long as a woman shall not burn herself after her husband's death, she shall be subject to transmigration in a female form." (9)

Hear too what Vishnoo [Vishnu, a seer] the saint says:

"After the death of her husband a wife must live as an ascetic, or ascend his pile." (10)

Now hear the words of the Bruhmu Pooran [Brahma Purana, a classic text] on the subject of Postcremation: "If her lord die in another country, let the faithful wife place his sandals on her breast, and pure enter the fire." (11)

The faithful widow is declared no suicide by this text of the Rig Ved [Veda]: "When three days of impurity are gone she obtained obsequies." (12)

Gotum says: "To a Brahmunee [female Brahman] after the death of her husband, Postcremation is not permitted. But to women of the other classes it is esteemed a chief duty." (13)

"Living let her benefit her husband; dying she commits suicide." (14)

"The woman of the Brahman tribe that follows her dead husband cannot, on account of her self-destruction, convey either herself or her husband to heaven." (15)

Concremation and Postcremation being thus established by the words of many sacred lawgivers, how can you say they are forbidden by the Shastrus, and desire to prevent their practice?

Opponent. All those passages you have quoted are indeed sacred law; and it is clear from those authorities, that if women perform Concremation or Postcremation, they will enjoy heaven for a considerable time. But attend to what Munoo [Manu, a sage] and others say respecting the duty of widows: "Let her emaciate her body, by living voluntarily on pure flowers, roots, and fruits, but let her not, when her lord is deceased, even pronounce the name of another man. Let her continue till death forgiving all injuries, performing harsh duties, avoiding every sensual pleasure, and cheerfully practising the incomparable rules of virtue which have been followed by such women as were devoted to one only husband." (16)

Here Munoo directs, that after the death of her husband, the widow should pass her whole life as an ascetic. Therefore, the laws given by Ungira and others whom you have quoted, being contrary to the law of Munoo, cannot be accepted; because the Ved declares, "Whatever Munoo has said is Wholesome;" (17) and Vrihusputi [Brihaspati, a sage], "Whatever law is contrary to the law of Munoo is not commendable." (18) The Ved especially declares, "By living in the practice of regular and occasional duties the mind may be purified. Thereafter by hearing, reflecting, and constantly meditating on the Supreme Being, absorption in Bruhmu may be attained. Therefore from a desire during life of future fruition, life ought not to be destroyed." (19) Munoo, Yagnyuvulkyu [Yagnavalkya, a sage] , and others, have then, in their respective codes of laws, prescribed to widows the duties of ascetics only. By this passage of the Ved, therefore, and the authority of Munoo and others, the words you have quoted from Ungira and the rest are set aside; for by the express declaration of the former, widows after the death of their husbands may, by living as ascetics, obtain absorption.

Advocate. What you have quoted from Munoo and Yagnyuvulkyu and the text of the Ved is admitted. But how can you set aside the following text of the Rig Ved on the subject of Concremation? "O fire! let these women, with bodies anointed with clarified butter, eyes coloured with collyrium, and void of tears, enter thee, the parent of water, that they may not be separated from their husbands, but may be, in unison with excellent husbands, themselves sinless and jewels amongst women." (20)

Opponent. This text of the Ved, and the former passages from Hareet and the rest whom you have quoted, all praise the practice of Concremation as leading the fruition, and are addressed to those who are occupied by sensual desires; and you cannot but admit that to follow these practices is only optional. In repeating the Sunkulpyu [sankalpa, conception] of Concremation, the desire of future fruition is declared as the object. The text therefore of the Ved which we have quoted, offering no gratifications, supersedes, in every respect, that which you have adduced, as well as all the words of Ungira and the rest. In proof we quote the text of the Kuthopunishud [Katha Upanishad]: "Faith in God which leads to absorption is one thing; and rites which have future fruition for their object, another. Each of these, producing different consequences, hold out to man inducements to follow it. The man, who of these two chooses faith, is blessed: and he, who for the sake of reward practices rites, is dashed away from the enjoyment of eternal beatitude." (21) Also the Moonduk Opunishud [Mudaka Upanishad]: "Rites, of which there are eighteen members, are all perishable: he who considers them as the source of blessing shall undergo repeated transmigrations; and all those fools who, immersed in the foolish practice of rites, consider themselves to be wise and learned, are repeatedly subjected to birth, disease, death, and other pains. When one blind man is guided by another, both subject themselves on their way to all kinds of distress." (22)

It is asserted in the Bhugvut Geeta [Bhagavad Gita[, the essence of all the Smritis [traditions], Poorans [Purana, compilations of texts], and Itahases [Itihasa, epic], that, "all those ignorant persons who attach themselves to the words of the Veds that convey promises of fruition, consider those falsely alluring passages as leading to real happiness, and say, that besides them there is no other reality. Agitated in their minds by these desires, they believe the abodes of the celestial gods to be the chief object; and they devote themselves to those texts which treat of ceremonies and their fruits, and entice by promises of employment. Such people can have no real confidence in the Supreme Being.' (23) Thus also do the Moonduk Opunishud and the Geeta state that, "the science by which a knowledge of God is attained is superior to all other knowledge:' (24) Therefore it is clear, from those passages of the Ved and of the Geeta, that the words of the Ved which promise fruition, are set aside by the texts of a contrary import. Moreover, the ancient saints and holy teachers, and their commentators; and yourselves, as well as we and all others, agree that Munoo is better acquainted than any other lawgiver with the spirit of the Ved. And he, understanding the meaning of those different texts, admitting the inferiority of that which promised fruition, and following that which conveyed no promise of gratifications, has directed widows to spend their lives as ascetics. He has also defined in his 12th chapter, what acts are observed merely for the sake of gratifications, and what are not. "Whatever act is performed for the sake of gratifications in this world or the next is called Pruburttuk, and those which are performed according to the knowledge respecting God, are called Niburtuk. All those who perform acts to procure gratifications, may enjoy heaven like the gods; and he who performs acts free from desires, procures release from the five elements of this body, that is, obtains absorption."

Advocate. Though what you have advanced from the Ved and sacred codes against the practice of Concremation and Postcremation, is not to be set aside, yet we have had the practice prescribed by Hareet and others handed down to us.

Opponent. Such an argument is highly inconsistent with justice. It is every way improper to persuade to self-destruction by citing passages of inadmissible authority. In the second place, it is evident from your own authorities, and the Sunkulpu recited in conformity with them, that the widow should voluntarily quit life, ascending the flaming pile of her husband. But, on the contrary, you first bind down the widow along with the corpse of her husband, and then heap over her such a quantity of wood that she cannot rise. At the time too of setting fire to the pile, you press her down with large bamboos. In what passage of Hareet or the rest do you find authority for thus binding the woman according to your practice? This then is, in fact, deliberate female murder.

Advocate. Though Hareet and the rest do not indeed authorize this practice of binding, &c., yet were a woman after having recited the Sunkulpu not to perform Concremation, it would be sinful, and considered disgraceful by others. It is on this account that we have adopted the custom.

Opponent. Respecting the sinfulness of such an act, that is mere talk: for in the same codes it is laid down, that the performance of a penance will obliterate the sin of quitting the pile. (30) Or in case of inability to undergo the regular penance, absolution may be obtained by bestowing the value of a cow, or three kahuns of cowries. Therefore the sin is no cause of alarm. The disgrace in the opinion of others is also nothing: for good men regard not the blame or reproach of persons who can reprobate those who abstain from the sinful murder of women. And do you not consider how great is the sin to kill a woman; therein forsaking the fear of God, the fear of conscience, and the fear of the Shastrus, merely from a dread of the reproach of those who delight in female murder?

Advocate. Though tying down in this manner be not authorized by the Shastrus, yet we practise it as being a custom that has been observed throughout Hindoosthan.

Opponent. It never was the case that the practice of fastening down widows on the pile was prevalent throughout Hindoosthan; for it is but of late years that this mode has been followed, and that only in Bengal, which is but a small part of Hindoosthan. No one besides who has the fear of God and man before him, will assert that male or female murder, theft &c., from having been long practised, cease to be vices. If, according to your argument, custom ought to set aside the precepts of the Shastrus, the inhabitants of the forests and mountains who have been in the habits of plunder, must be considered as guiltless of sin, and it would be improper to endeavour to restrain their habits. The Shastrus, and the reasonings connected with them, enable us to discriminate right and wrong. In those Shastrus such female murder is altogether forbidden. And reason also declares, that to bind down a woman for her destruction, holding out to her the inducement of heavenly rewards, is a most sinful act.

Advocate. This practice may be sinful or any thing else, but we will not refrain from observing it. Should it cease, people would generally apprehend that if women did not perform Concremation on the death of their husbands, they might go astray; but if they burn themselves this fear is done away. Their families and relations are freed from apprehension. And if the husband could be assured during his life that his wife would follow him on the pile, his mind would be at ease from apprehensions of her misconduct.

Opponent. What can be done, if, merely to avoid the possible danger of disgrace, you are unmercifully resolved to commit the sin of female murder. But is there not also a danger of a woman's going astray during the lifetime of her husband, particularly when he resides for a long time in a distant country? What remedy then have you got against this cause of alarm?

Advocate. There is a great difference betwixt the case of the husband's being alive, and of his death; for while a husband is alive, whether he resides near or at a distance, a wife is under his control; she must stand in awe of him. But after his death that authority ceases, and she of course is divested of fear.

Opponent. The Shastrus which command that a wife should live under the control of her husband during his life, direct that on his death she shall live under the authority of her husband's family, or else under that of her parental relations; and the Shastrus have authorized the ruler of the country to maintain the observance of this law. Therefore, the possibility of a woman's going astray cannot be more guarded against during the husband's life than it is after his death. For you daily see, that even while the husband is alive, he gives up his authority, and the life separates from him. Control alone cannot restrain from evil thoughts, words, and actions; but the suggestions of wisdom and the fear of God may cause both man and woman to abstain from sin. Both the Shastrus and experience show this.

Advocate. You have repeatedly asserted, that from want of feeling we promote female destruction. This is incorrect, for it is declared in our Ved and codes of law, that mercy is the root of virtue, and from our practice of hospitality, &c. our compassionate dispositions are well known.

Opponent. That in other cases you shew charitable dispositions is acknowledged. But by witnessing from your youth the voluntary burning of women amongst your elder relatives, your neighbours and the inhabitants of the surrounding villages, and by observing the indifference manifested at the time when the women are writhing under the torture of the flames, habits of insensibility are produced. For the same reason, when men or women are suffering the pains of death, you feel for them no sense of compassion, like the worshippers of the female deities who, witnessing from their infancy the slaughter of kids and buffaloes, feel no compassion for them in the time of their suffering death, while followers of Vishnoo [the god Vishnu] are touched with strong feelings of pity.

Advocate. What you have said I shall carefully consider.

Opponent. It is to me a source of great satisfaction, that you are now ready to take this matter into your consideration. By forsaking prejudice and reflecting on the Shastru, what is really conformable to its precepts may be perceived, and the evils and disgrace brought on this country by the crime of female murder will cease.

✧ Govinda Samanta ✧

Lal Behari Day

The British Parliament assumed control over the East India Company and its territories by the charter reforms in 1813 and 1833 and finally dissolved it. As described in the introduction to the text by Ram Mohan Roy, the Company had been made responsible for public education in 1813, setting off a long debate over the content, language to be used, extent, and government role in schooling. The debate ended with a decision in 1835 that the government would emphasize higher education in English with a Western curriculum. The British assumed that educated Indians would become teachers and that education would reach the masses through "downward filtration"; in fact, educated Indians preferred careers in the professions and government service rather than teaching. As a result, primary education was neglected and by 1844 there were only eleven government secondary schools and forty primary schools throughout India that taught using the English language—many fewer than the vernacular schools (which used the local literary language) that had appeared privately and through missionary effort.

In the course of this debate, the Company conducted several studies of indigenous education in the 1820s. It found that local schools were widespread and very popular. Some British observers claimed that Indian education, particularly in Bengal, was superior to European education for the lower classes. These schools declined through lack of support from the government and from competition with missionary schools.

Half a century after Ram Mohan Roy, Lal Behari Day (1824–1894) was one of the few Indian scholars who devoted his career to teaching. He converted to Christianity in 1843 at the missionary school he attended and was ordained a missionary in 1855. He left the ministry in 1867 and joined the government Educational Service; he taught English literature, history, and philosophy until he retired in 1889. In 1872 he won a £50 prize in a contest for a novel written about Bengali rural life. Published two years later, *Govinda Samanta, or the History of a Bengal Raiyat*, is less a novel, however, than a series of episodes about Bengali villages centered around the life of Govinda from his birth to his death.

Day writes in his introduction, "The reader is to expect here a plain and unvarnished tale of a plain peasant, living in this plain country of Bengal," but he is being disingenuous. The book is a carefully constructed critique of British colonialism. For example, Day reacts to the derogatory comments on Indian civilization by such people as James Mill. Mill (who never visited India) was examiner of correspondence for the East India Company; he drafted dispatches to India and read all the replies to them. This job qualified him as a leading expert on India, a role that he put to good use in his multivolume *History of India* (1818). One of the aims of this book was to dispel the "sentimental" admiration for Indian civilization; he wrote that Indians tolerated filth in a childlike manner. Even those British who recognized the sanitary and hygienic aspects of Indian preoccupation with purity and pollution accepted this notion. In *Govinda Samanta*, Day responds with obsessively detailed descriptions of the cleanliness of the villagers.

In the excerpts below, the focus is on traditional village education, which is being supplanted by state-regulated schools. The British Parliament made the East India Company responsible for mass education in the territories it ruled in 1813, and required the Company to admit Christian missionaries. The missions built schools in the belief that Western education would encourage conversion. After 1854 missionary schools received grants-in-aid from the government, while the government opened three universities that provided education in English. As a mission-educated teacher and minister, Day was a contributor both to the Western content of the curriculum and to the Christianizing mission of schools. In his book he tries to strike a balance between the positive and negative aspects of the traditional school system. This episode is set in the mid-1850s, but the details are very similar to those in the reports made for the East India Company in the 1820s and probably more accurately resemble the schools of that period.

Questions

1. What are the advantages and disadvantages of this form of education over English schools? Does it seem to be more suited to the needs of Bengali villagers, as the author claims?
2. Day says that Kanchanpur had 1,500 residents and thirty-six castes. From the information in the text, how widespread would you estimate was schooling in this village?
3. Does the author approve of corporal punishment? Do you?
4. What aspects of Western civilization would Day agree with Ram Mohan Roy were beneficial? What would they disagree about?

Govinda Samanta

Lal Behari Day

Lal Behari Day, *Govinda Samanta, or the History of a Bengal Raiyat* (London: Macmillan, 1874), pp. 69, 71–78, 112–117, 123–125

The day on which Govinda was for the first time taken to the *pāṭhśālā* [school] was an important day to the family, as well as to our hero himself. Though, unlike the middle and higher classes, who seldom send a child to school for the first time without performing some religious ceremonies, the poorer classes ask not the ministrations of the Brahman [priestly caste], yet the matter is regarded with the liveliest interest. Ever since his birth, Govinda has not had a stitch of clothing on his person; though more than five years old, he was allowed to revel in the unrestrained freedom of primaeval nudity. It was on the morning of that important day that his grandmother wrapped round his waist, in folds, the *dhuti* [loincloth] of which I have spoken, leaving the rest of the body—which was nearly the whole—quite naked. Thus dressed, our little man bowed down to the ground before his grandmother, his mother, his father, uncles, and aunt, and they all gave him their benedictions. As on the very first day he was expected at the *pāṭhśālā* to commence writing, Badan [Govinda's father] tied in one corner of Govinda's *dhuti*, a piece of chalk, or rather *rāmkhadi*, [mineral used for chalk]. . . .

. . . in the middle of the village of Kanchanpur, there are two temples of Siva facing each other, and that one of those temples has before it a colonnade. In this colonnade was held the village *pāṭhśālā*, properly so called, where the sons of Brahmans, Kayasthas [scribe caste], and wealthy bankers received instruction from a Brahman *gurumahāśaya*. This *gurumahāśaya*, or *mahāśaya*—as he is usually called in the Burdwan district—belonged to a race of hereditary pedagogues, since his father, grandfather, great-grandfather, and all his ancestors up to the fourteenth generation backwards, were the schoolmasters of the village. There was in the village, however, another pedagogue whose school bore to the other one the same relation which a dissenting chapel in England bears to the parish church. He occupied a far inferior social position: indeed he was not a Brahman, but a Kayastha, and therefore obtained only a third part of the pupils of the other. Any day you might have seen in the school of the Brahman pedagogue between sixty and seventy boys, whereas in the other school you seldom saw more than twenty. And yet the Brahman was by no means a better teacher than the Kayastha. The former, though he had read a part of the *Saṅkshipta-Sāra*—the Sanskrit grammar in vogue in the Vardhamana district—and would repeat a lot of Sanskrit *ślokas* with which his conversation was interlarded, yet made ludicrous mistakes in Bengali orthography; the latter made no pretensions to Sanskrit scholarship, but was universally acknowledged to be an arithmetician of the first water; and he was strong in zamindari [landholder] accounts, a subject of which the Brahman *mahāśaya* had no knowledge. Though the school of the Kayastha teacher was attended chiefly by the lower castes and the poorer classes, there was amongst them a sprinkling of Brahman boys, particularly those whose parents wished to give them a mathematical education and an insight into the mysteries of zamindari accounts. Badan preferred the Kayastha to the Brahman teacher for two reasons:—first, because the school of the latter was the more aristocratic of the two, and he wished his son to be educated along with those who were his equals in social position, or at any rate, not very much higher, and secondly, because he wanted Govinda to learn zamindari accounts. Accordingly Badan and Govinda proceeded to the house of Rama Rupa Sarkara (for that was the name of the Kayastha pedagogue), who held his school in the yard of his house. . . .

"Well, Badan, what is the news? what brings you here?" asked Rama Rupa seated on a mat before about a dozen pupils variously engaged in writing on paper, or plantain-leaf or palm-leaf.

Badan. "You see, *mahāśaya*, this boy of mine; I wish to put him under you, that you may make a man of him."

Rama. "Well done! Badan! You wish your son taught *lekhá-pąda* [reading and writing], a thing you don't know yourself! Well, you are right. The poet Chanakya says—*Vidyāratna mahadhanam*, that is to say, learning or education is a great treasure."

Badan. "Yes, sir, that's quite true. A man who cannot read and write is a truly poor man—he is blind. Though I have two eyes, I am really blind, for I cannot read what is written on a bit of paper."

Rama. "Badan, you had better sit down, and smoke. Modo! go and make tobacco ready."

Badan sat down on the bare ground, Govinda stood near him, and Madhu, one of the advanced pupils of the school, went away to get tobacco and fire for his teacher. In Bengal, and I suppose in other parts of India, pupils, especially in the villages, do, without a grudge, even menial services for their teacher; indeed, they regard it as an honourable distinction to be so employed. Turning to Govinda, the *mahāśaya* said, "Well, my little man, so you want to be a *Panḍit* [scholar]. Come near me." Poor Govinda trembled from head to foot. He had heard from boys of his own age that every schoolmaster was a second Yama or Rhadamanthus, and every school a place where boys were unmercifully flogged. He therefore hesitated to go near Rama Rupa; but Badan shoved him forwards to the pedagogue, who patted him on the head and told him to be a good boy, and not to be afraid of his teacher. One of the advanced pupils was then ordered to trace on the ground the first five letters of the Bengali alphabet. Badan took out the *rāmkhadi* from his boy's clothes, and put it into his hand. Rama Rupa took hold of Govinda's hand, with the chalk in it, and led it over all the letters traced on the ground. In the meantime, the advanced pupil, Madhu, brought the hookah reeking with the fragrant weed, and put it into the hands of Rama Rupa. As Badan and Rama Rupa were of different castes, they could not smoke in the same hookah. The latter therefore gave to the former the earthen cup called *kalki*, which contains the tobacco and the fire, and Badan grasped the lower part of it with both his hands, and smoked away through the opening between the thumb and the forefinger of his right hand. After he had smoked two or three minutes he returned the *kalki* to the *mahāśaya*, who began to puff away with great zest. As the redoubtable pedagogue of Kanchanpur, now in the act of smoking, is in a state of repose—and tobacco, they say, is a wonderful sedative—we shall make an attempt to photograph his likeness, which is not always practicable, especially when, urged by a tempest of passion—as was frequently the case—his body trembles in every inch with rage, and his cane descends, thump after thump, with electric rapidity, on the backs of his unfortunate pupils. From the form of one of his legs, and the position in which it was put, you might have inferred that he was lame, and the inference would have been confirmed by the sight of a crutch that lay beside him. His lameness, to say the truth, was of no ordinary kind; he could with difficulty go, with the help of his crutch, from one room of his house to another; and, as for going out into the street, he scarcely went out even once in six months. Owing to this bodily defect, he was always called *khoṇḍa mahāśaya*, that is, the lame schoolmaster, in contra-distinction to the Brahman pedagogue. His pupils often lent him a helping hand in going from room to room, and sometimes, I am sorry to say, assisted him to a fall, as a sort of retaliation for the caning they so frequently received from him. He was about forty years old, had a dark skin, a spare body, an aquiline nose, and a rather high forehead for a Bengali. He stooped a great deal. In addition to his lameness, he had another bodily defect, which considerably marred his influence, and made him often an object of derision—he spoke through his nose. . . . His nasal twang was so strong, that, if he were speaking at night in a dark room, he might be mistaken by children for a ghost—for Bengali ghosts speak strongly through the nose.

But though a hopeless cripple as regards his body, and ghost-like in his speech, Rama Rupa had natural talents of no mean order. He was the first mathematician in the village. . . . But Rama Rupa was not only mathematical, he was eminently logical. Though he had not read the Sutras of Gotama [Buddha], he was an acute reasoner. Whenever the Christian missionary of Vardhamana came to the village in the course of his itineracy, he did not fail to pay a visit to the lame schoolmaster, who had many a tough argument with him; and the villagers always thought that the missionary was invariably worsted. . . .

Rama Rupa was a strict disciplinarian. He had by him constantly, besides his crutch, a thin but longish twig of bamboo, which often resounded, not only on the palms of his pupils' hands, but on their heads and backs; and sometimes also with cruel ingenuity he used to strike their knuckles, their knee-joints, and their ankles. You could hardly pass by the door of the house during school hours without hearing the *shop-a-shop, shop-a-shop* of the bamboo switch. But he had other ways of administering discipline. One famous mode of juvenile punishment was called *naḍu-Gopāl*, that is, Gopal (the god Krishna) with a sweetmeat in his hand. This consisted in making a boy sit on the ground with one leg in a kneeling posture; the two arms were then stretched, and a large brick was placed on each. In this posture a boy is expected to remain still for several hours. Should either of the bricks fall from the hand, down comes the bamboo switch on the pate of the delinquent. We shall mention only one other clause in Rama Rupa's penal code. The juvenile offender was handcuffed, and his feet were tied by strings to the trunk of the jack tree of which we have spoken. While the boy thus stood handcuffed and chained, the leaves of a stinging plant called *bichhuti* (Tragia involucrataj) were applied to different parts of his body. Whoever has been stung by a wasp or a hornet can have some idea of the sensation produced by the application of *bichhuti* to the skin. The agony is intense: perfectly helpless, unable to run away, unable even to stroke with his hand the part stung, the boy can do nothing but shriek. In justice to the lame schoolmaster of Kanchanpur, I should here remark that the above disciplinary process was not the product of his own fertile brain; it is a time-honoured institution which has been handed down from generation to generation of Bengali village schoolmasters. A few words on Rama Rupa's finances will conclude this chapter. The schooling fee was, on the average, one *anna* (a penny and halfpenny) a month per boy. Supposing he had thirty or thirty-two boys—I don't believe he ever had more—his monthly income would amount to two rupees, or four shillings. Besides this, he had a system of "requisitions." Most of the boys, when they came to the afternoon school—for the school was held first from early in the morning till about eleven o'clock, and again from three o'clock in the afternoon till candlelight—brought from their houses for their teacher either a betel-leaf, or a betel-nut, or a small ball of tobacco. In addition to these daily donations, every boy was expected to give to the *mahāśaya,* once a month, a *sidā*, which consisted of a quantity of unboiled rice, with a suitable accompaniment of vegetables, split pulse, mustard oil, salt, and even clarified butter. All this, no doubt, made a considerable addition to his income of four shillings a month, yet it was quite insufficient to support the pedagogue, his wife and two children; the deficiency was supplied by the produce of about ten *bighā*s [about three acres] of land which, as he was unable to cultivate them himself, he held in partnership with a neighbouring husbandman. . . .

We must now return to our hero, and notice what progress he was making in reading and writing under that redoubtable pedagogue, Rama

Rupa Sarkar, of Kanchanpur. We saw him on the first day trace his letters with chalk on the ground; he remained at it for about six months, after which he exchanged the ground for palmyra-leaves, and chalk for the reed and ink. . . . As for the writing material, slates were unknown, till they were introduced into the country by the English, and are used only in schools organised on the English model. The leaves of the fan-palm are preferable to slates for beginners, for three reasons:—in the *first* place, the palm-leaf costs nothing, especially in the villages; *secondly*, it is more lasting, as it never breaks, and seldom tears; *thirdly*, it is lighter than a slate, and therefore can be more easily carried by children. Provided with a bundle of about twenty pieces of the palmyra-leaf under his left arm, the reed-pen resting on the upper hollow of his right ear, an earthen ink-pot in his left hand, and his right hand free, our hero used every morning and afternoon to go to the *pāṭhśālā*, with other boys of the neighbourhood. He always returned home with his hands, face, and *dhuti* bespattered with ink; for whenever he wrote on the palm-leaf a wrong letter or an ill-formed one, he immediately used to brush it off with his hand, or his wrist. But Alanga [Govinda's father's mother] and Sundari [his mother] were rather pleased with the sight than otherwise, for the abundance of ink on his body and clothes only showed how diligent their darling was in his studies.

In the old-fashioned, orthodox village *pāṭhśālā*, which are even now found all over the country, a boy only writes for some years, and does a little arithmetic, but seldom reads a book, the two subjects to which the greatest attention is paid being calligraphy and arithmetic. Early in the morning, when Govinda went to school, he spent some hours in writing the fifty letters of the Bengali alphabet, the compound letters which are so puzzling to foreigners, the numerals from one to a hundred, and the like. Before the forenoon school was dismissed he recited, in a chorus with other boys, those compound letters and the numerals. In the afternoon school he again wrote those very things, and in the evening, before being dismissed, recited in a sing-song manner, along with other boys, the whole of the Multiplication Table up to twenty times twenty, a table with which Bengali boys are more familiar than any other boys in the world. Next to the writing of the alphabet followed the writing of proper names, especially of persons; the names of all the boys in the school, and those of the major part of the inhabitants of the village successively, appeared on the stage of the palm-leaf.

The study of arithmetic went on *pari passu* with calligraphy and orthography. First came a lot of arithmetical tables, which were all committed to memory; addition, both simple and compound, followed; next, subtraction, both simple and compound; then the boy at once passed on—for Bengali arithmetic has not the formal processes of multiplication and division—to what in European arithmetic is called Proportion, or the Rule of Three [an ancient Indian form of cross-multiplication], but which in Bengali goes by the various names *serkashā*, *mankashā*, *kānchānāmāshā*, *sudkashā* (interest), *kāthākāli*, *bighākāli* (mensuration), according to the subjects to which the doctrine of Proportion is applied. The reader must not suppose that Govinda went through this course of arithmetic; his school course was cut short, as we shall see by-and-by, after he had mastered compound subtraction. As slates are not used in the village schools, and black-boards are as unknown in the *pāṭhśālā* as Babbage's Calculating Machine, and as palm-leaves are ill adapted for containing long rows of figures, all arithmetical operations are carried on, at least for some years in a boy's school life, on the mud floor of the schoolhouse.

The lowest class of a Bengali *pāṭhśālā*, of the primitive orthodox fashion, is the chalk or *floor class*; in this class Govinda remained about six months. The next class is the palm-leaf class, in which our hero studied for about three years. In the beginning of his fourth year he was promoted to the plantain-leaf class. Higher than the plantain-leaf class is the paper class, in which boys write on paper instead of on plantain-leaves; but Govinda's education did not come up so high. His education ended in the plantain-leaf class, of which some detailed account may not be unacceptable to the reader. Govinda now threw away his palm-leaves, and took to the plantain, of the leaves of which he had an abundant supply in his own house; but if the supply was now and then exhausted in consequence of the celebration of a feast, on which occasion plantain-leaves do, as we have seen, the duty of plates, he had only to beg or borrow, or to steal them from neighbouring houses or gardens. Govinda now gave up the writing of merely personal names, and took to epistolary composition. This same study of epistolary composition, or correspondence, is a most important branch of Bengali education, and is pursued for years in the village *pāṭhśālā*. Essay-writing is unknown in the primitive schools of Bengal, simply because it is not necessary to the purposes of life. Whatever is required in practical life is assiduously studied; and it must be acknowledged that the writing of letters is of essential importance to persons engaged in business. Nor is Bengali letter-writing an easy task.

There are hundreds of set forms in which men are to be addressed according to their station in life, and to the relations in which they stand to the writer. The form in which the writer of a letter should address his father is different from that in which he should address his uncle, and the paternal uncle different from that in which he should address his maternal uncle; and the same is true of all the degrees of consanguinity and relationship; so that the set forms of epistolary address are practically infinite. On this dark and unfathomable ocean of epistolary composition our hero was now launched.

By the way, our English schools and colleges in Bengal might take a hint in this respect from the village *pāṭhśālā*. Our educated young men, our B.A.s and M.A.s in general, can hardly write a common letter in every-day English. They will write you a long Essay on the Feudal System in Europe, or a critique on "Macbeth," or an analysis of "The Flower and the Leaf"; but they will murder the Queen's English in writing a common business letter. There must be something vicious, something essentially wrong, in such a system of education. Of the two systems, the system of the village *pāṭhśālā*, which aims at the practical and the useful, is infinitely more sensible. By all means have the ornamental part of education, but do not sacrifice utility to ornament. An M.A. and Fellow of the Calcutta University, when joining his appointment at a Mofussil Station, thus notified his arrival to his official superior: "Sir, I beg to inform you that I have arrived here yesterday." *O tempora! O mores*! Can nothing be done to remedy this disgraceful state of things?

It may be easily believed that our hero was often subjected to that system of disciplinary correction of which Rama Rupa was so warm an advocate. A peasant's son, young, vigorous, and in rude health, Govinda hated the restraints of a school, and often played the truant. Instead of going to school he often repaired to the high embankment of some distant tank, or to some mango tope or tamarind grove, and there played with boys tending cattle. Rama Rupa, however, adopted vigorous measures for the seizing of truants. He had formed a sort of detective police, consisting of four able-bodied *sardārpoḍos*, or senior pupils, who were sent out whenever a truant had to be caught. Whenever Govinda was absent from school, these detectives went to his house, and asked his mother or grandmother where he was. If told that he had gone to school as usual, they sought for him in the outskirts of the village, and especially his favourite haunts, and invariably captured him. If he showed resistance, his legs would be caught hold of by two of the lads, and his arms by the other two. Thus suspended between four stout bearers, Govinda, half dead with fright, was often brought to the *pāṭhśālā*, and there well thrashed by the pedagogue. This detective police was useful to the village schoolmaster in other ways. Whenever there was a feast in his house—and feasts are ever and anon occurring in Hindu houses, however poor—and he stood in need of plantain-leaves, to serve as plates for his guests, he had only to order his detectives to procure them; and they forthwith entered some garden and stole plantain-leaves for their teacher, who, asking no question for conscience sake, gladly received them with thanks. . . . Badan, Kālamnik, and Gayārām, [Badan's younger brothers] generally spent their evenings at home . . . and after they had washed their feet and hands, they spread a mat in the court-yard, sat upon it cross-legged, smoked, and talked on the events of the day. Alanga often sat near them, not on the mat, but on the ground at a little distance, and joined in the conversation. The subjects of conversation were often the state of the weather; bullocks; the progress made in ploughing, or harrowing, or sowing, or irrigating; the zamindar's rent; and the *mahājan*'s (money-lender's) INTEREST. In all these matters old Alanga took as keen an interest as Badan himself. Sometimes a neighbour dropped in, to whom was administered the never-failing hospitality of the hookah.

Govinda was invariably present at these evening-parties. At sun-down, he returned from the *pāṭhśālā*; put away in a corner of the verandah of the big hut his bundle of palmyra-leaves, his reed-pen, and earthen pot of ink; washed his hands, feet, and mouth, at the tank; ate in the kitchen his dāl and bhāt [lentils and rice], dealt to him either by his mother or his grandmother—for, as a little boy, he could not wait so late as eight or nine o'clock, when the men and the women (excepting Alanga, who, as a widow, had only one meal), usually had their supper: and sat on the mat in the yard beside his father and uncles. Sitting there he was made to recite the Multiplication Table, and other lessons which he had learnt at school. Badan, though not initiated into the mysteries of reading and writing, often put arithmetical questions to his son and heir. The following are specimens of the questions he put:

"If for one pice you get ten plantains, how many plantains would you get for four pice?"

"If for one pice you get ten plantains, what would be the price of fifty plantains?"

The first time Badan proposed such questions, Govinda in his simplicity, asked, “Which sort of plantains, *Bābā*? (*Bābā*, being invariably used in Bengali for papa.) Is it the *martamāna*, or the *kāntāli* kind?”

Badan, giving a smile significant of superior wisdom, sagely replied, “It does not matter, Govin, what sort of plantain it is, the calculation is all the same.”

Over a question, Govinda would sometimes spend a quarter of an hour, and Badan, fearing that the little mathematician had fallen asleep, would ask, “Are you sleeping, Govin? when Govinda would immediately answer, “No, Baba, I am not sleeping; I am calculating it in my mind.”

✧ Gitanjali ✧

Rabindranath Tagore

Rabindranath Tagore (1861–1941) was one of the giants of South Asian literature, and his works occupy a permanent place in the hearts of the Bengalis. A Nobel laureate poet, author, and philosopher, he was the ambassador of Indian culture to the rest of the world. In 1913, Tagore became the first Asian person to be awarded the Nobel Prize, for his collection of poems titled *Gitanjali* (song offerings). He was first of all a poet, but his talents went far beyond his poetry; he produced notable contributions in different branches of art, including novels, short stories, dramas, articles, essays, paintings, and music. The national anthems of two countries, India and Bangladesh, are taken from his work. He was a social reformer, patriot, and, above all, a great humanitarian and philosopher.

Tagore was born in Calcutta on May 7, 1861, into a wealthy family. His grandfather Dwarakanath Tagore was a rich landlord and social reformer whose home was a center of culture. Largely home-schooled, the boy published his first poem anonymously at the age of thirteen. His first book of poems, *Kabi Kahini* (tale of a poet) was published in 1878. In the same year he traveled to England and was admitted into University College London. In 1880 Tagore returned to India, where he continued to write poetry and musical plays.

In 1890, he went to Shilaidaha (now in Bangladesh) to look after his family estate. Here, Tagore was influenced by the natural beauty and simple but elegant life of rural Bengal. This became a consistent theme in his subsequent works. In 1909 he began writing *Gitanjali* and in 1912 journeyed to Europe for a second time. On the trip to London he translated some of the poems and songs from *Gitanjali* into English. The India Society of London published *Gitanjali*, containing 103 translated poems, in 1913; William B. Yeats wrote the introduction for the volume. The book created a sensation in the literary world. Tagore, who was traveling in America at the time, delivered lectures in Rochester, Boston, and Harvard University. Upon his return to India and his winning of the Nobel Prize for literature, the University of Calcutta conferred on him the honorary degree of doctor of letters (D.Litt.).

In addition to his literary contributions, Tagore participated in the Indian nationalist movement, though in his own visionary way. He was at the vortex of the political storm that gathered over India in the first decade of the twentieth century. Gandhi, the political father of modern India, was his devoted friend. The ruling British government knighted Tagore in 1915, but he resigned the honor a few years later as a protest against the Amritsar massacre (Jallianwallah Bagh), when British soldiers killed at least 1,526 unarmed civilians.

The excerpt below, which contains the first thirty-two poems from the English translation of *Gitanjali*, offers a fair sampling of the beauty and simplicity of the work. Preceding the poems and songs is the introduction by Yeats mentioned above. It captures the excitement and acclaim that *Gitanjali* and Tagore inspired in the West. While only a brief background of the work and its author is possible here, more biographical information, images, and paintings can be found at http://www.calcuttaweb.com/tagore.

Questions

1. The relationship between an individual and God is a subject that runs throughout the readings contained in this volume. How would you describe this relationship in *Gitanjali*?
2. How do the poems in *Gitanjali* describe how one can find God?
3. What forges the chains that imprison an individual? How does one break these bonds?
4. Does the union between an individual and God in *Gitanjali* suggest any other type of union? If so, what?

Gitanjali

Rabindranath Tagore, *Gitanjali: Song Offerings*[1]
(London: Macmillan, 1913), pp. vii–xxii, 1–27

Introduction

A few days ago I said to a distinguished Bengali doctor of medicine, "I know no German, yet if a translation of a German poet had moved me, I would go to the British Museum and find books in English that would tell me something of his life, and of the history of his thought. But though these prose translations from Rabindranath Tagore have stirred my blood as nothing has for years, I shall not know anything of his life, and of the movements of thought that have made them possible, if some Indian traveller will not tell me." It seemed to him natural that I should be moved, for he said, "I read Rabindranath every day, to read one line of his is to forget all the troubles of the world." I said, "An Englishman living in London in the reign of Richard the Second had he been shown translations from Petrarch or from Dante, would have found no books to answer his questions, but would have questioned some Florentine banker or Lombard merchant as I question you. For all I know, so abundant and simple is this poetry, the new renaissance has been born in your country and I shall never know of it except by hearsay." He answered, "We have other poets, but none that are his equal; we call this the epoch of Rabindranath. No poet seems to me as famous in Europe as he is among us. He is as great in music as in poetry, and his songs are sung from the west of India into Burma wherever Bengali is spoken. He was already famous at nineteen when he wrote his first novel; and plays when he was but little older, are still played in Calcutta. I so much admire the completeness of his life; when he was very young he wrote much of natural objects, he would sit all day in his garden; from his twenty-fifth year or so to his thirty-fifth perhaps, when he had a great sorrow, he wrote the most beautiful love poetry in our language"; and then he said with deep emotion, "words can never express what I owed at seventeen to his love poetry.

---

[1] A collection of prose translations made by the author from the original Bengali. With an introduction by W.B. Yeats.

After that his art grew deeper, it became religious and philosophical; all the inspiration of mankind are in his hymns. He is the first among our saints who has not refused to live, but has spoken out of Life itself, and that is why we give him our love." I may have changed his well-chosen words in my memory but not his thought. "A little while ago he was to read divine service in one of our churches—we of the Brahma Samaj use your word "church" in English—it was the largest in Calcutta and not only was it crowded, but the streets were all but impassable because of the people."

Other Indians came to see me and their reverence for this man sounded strange in our world, where we hide great and little things under the same veil of obvious comedy and half-serious depreciation. When we were making the cathedrals had we a like reverence for our great men? "Every morning at three—I know, for I have seen it"—one said to me, "he sits immovable in contemplation, and for two hours does not awake from his reverie upon the nature of God. His father, the Maha Rishi, would sometimes sit there all through the next day; once, upon a river, he fell into contemplation because of the beauty of the landscape, and the rowers waited for eight hours before they could continue their journey." He then told me of Mr. Tagore's family and how for generations great men have come out of its cradles. "Today," he said, "there are Gogonendranath and Abanindranath Tagore, who are artists; and Dwijendranath, Rabindranath's brother, who is a great philosopher. The squirrels come from the boughs and climb on to his knees and the birds alight upon his hands." I notice in these men's thought a sense of visible beauty and meaning as though they held that doctrine of Nietzsche that we must not believe in the moral or intellectual beauty which does not sooner or later impress itself upon physical things. I said, "In the East you know how to keep a family illustrious. The other day the curator of a museum pointed out to me a little dark-skinned man who was arranging their Chinese prints and said, "That is the hereditary connoisseur of the Mikado, he is the fourteenth of his family to hold the post." He answered, "When Rabindranath was a boy he had all round him in his home literature and music." I thought of the abundance, of the simplicity of the poems, and said, "In your country is there much propagandist writing, much criticism? We have to do so much, especially in my own country, that our minds gradually cease to be creative, and yet we cannot help it. If our life was not a continual warfare, we would not have taste, we would not know what is good, we would not find hearers and readers. Four-fifths of our energy is spent in the quarrel with bad taste, whether in our own minds or in the minds of others." "I understand," he replied, "we too have our propagandist writing. In the villages they recite long mythological poems adapted from the Sanskrit in the Middle Ages, and they often insert passages telling the people that they must do their duties."

I have carried the manuscript of these translations about with me for days, reading it in railway trains, or on the top of omnibuses and in restaurants, and I have often had to close it lest some stranger would see how much it moved me. These lyrics—which are in the original, my Indians tell me, full of subtlety of rhythm, of untranslatable delicacies of colour, of metrical invention—display in their thought a world I have dreamed of all my life long. The work of a supreme culture, they yet appear as much the growth of the common soil as the grass and the rushes. A tradition, where poetry and religion are the same thing, has passed through the centuries, gathering from learned and unlearned metaphor and emotion, and carried back again to the multitude the thought of the scholar and of the noble. If the civilization of Bengal remains unbroken, if that common mind which—as one divines—runs through all, is not, as with us, broken into a dozen minds that know nothing of each other, something even of what is most subtle in these verses will have come, in a few generations, to the beggar on the roads. When there was but one mind in England, Chaucer wrote his *Troilus and Cressida*, and thought he had written to be read, or to be read out—for our time was coming on apace—he was sung by minstrels for a while. Rabindranath Tagore, like Chaucer's forerunners, writes music for his words, and one understands at every moment that he is so abundant, so spontaneous, so daring in his passion, so full of surprise, because he is doing something which has never seemed strange, unnatural, or in need of defence. These verses will not lie in little well-printed books upon ladies' tables, who turn the pages with indolent hands that they may sigh over a life without meaning, which is yet all they can know of life, or be carried by students at the university to be laid aside when the work of life begins, but, as the generations pass, travellers will hum them on the highway and men rowing upon the rivers. Lovers, while they await one another, shall find, in murmuring them, this love of God a magic gulf wherein their own more bitter passion may bathe and renew its youth. At every moment the heart of this poet flows outward to these without derogation or condescension, for it has known that they will understand; and it has filled itself with the circumstance of their lives. The traveller in the red-brown clothes that he wears that dust may not show upon him, the girl searching in her bed for the petals fallen from the wreath of her royal lover, the servant or the bride awaiting the master's home-coming in the empty house, are images of the heart turning to God. Flowers and rivers, the blowing of conch shells, the heavy rain of the Indian July, or the moods of that heart in union or in separation; and a man sitting in a boat upon a river playing a lute, like one of those figures full of mysterious meaning in a Chinese picture, is God Himself. A whole people, a whole civilization, immeasurably strange to us, seems to have been taken up into this imagination; and yet we are not moved because of its strangeness, but because we have met our own image, as though we had walked in Rossetti's willow wood, or heard, perhaps for the first time in literature, our voice as in a dream.

Since the Renaissance the writing of European saints—however familiar their metaphor and the general structure of their thought—has ceased to hold our attention. We know that we must at last forsake the world, and we are accustomed in moments of weariness or exaltation to consider a voluntary forsaking; but how can we, who have read so much poetry, seen so many paintings, listened to so much music, where the cry of the flesh and the cry of the soul seems one, forsake it harshly and rudely? What have we in common with St. Bernard covering his eyes that they may not dwell upon the beauty of the lakes of Switzerland, or with the violent rhetoric of the Book of Revelations? We would, if we might, find, as in this book, words full of courtesy. "I have got my leave. Bid me farewell, my brothers! I bow to you all and take my departure. Here I give back the keys of my door—and I give up all claims to my house. I only ask for last kind words from you. We were neighbours for long, but I received more than I could give. Now the day has dawned and the lamp that lit my dark corner is out. A summons has come and I am ready for my journey." And it is our own mood, when it is furthest from à Kempis or John of the Cross, that cries, "And because I love this life, I know I shall love death as well." Yet it is not only in our thoughts of the parting that this book fathoms all. We had not known that we loved God, hardly it may be that we believed in Him; yet looking backward upon our life we discover, in our exploration of the pathways of woods, in our delight in the lonely places of hills, in that mysterious claim that we have made, unavailingly on the woman that we have loved, the emotion that created this insidious sweetness. "Entering my heart unbidden even as one of the common crowd, unknown to me, my king, thou didst press the signet of eternity upon many a fleeting moment." This is no longer the sanctity of the cell and of the scourge; being but a lifting up, as it were, into a greater intensity of the mood of the painter, painting the dust and the sunlight, and we go for a like voice to St. Francis and to William Blake who have seemed so alien in our violent history.

We write long books where no page perhaps has any quality to make writing a pleasure, being confident in some general design, just as we fight and make money and fill our heads with politics—all dull things in the doing—while Mr. Tagore, like the Indian civilization itself, has been content to discover the soul and surrender himself to its spontaneity. He often seems to contrast life with that of those who have loved more after our fashion, and have more seeming weight in the world, and always humbly as though he were only sure his way is best for him: "Men going home glance at me and smile and fill me with shame. I sit like a beggar maid, drawing my skirt over my face, and when they ask me, what it is I want, I drop my eyes and answer them not." At another time, remembering how his life had once a different shape, he will say, "Many an hour I have spent in the strife of the good and the evil, but now it is the pleasure of my playmate of the empty days to draw my heart on to him; and I know not why this sudden call to what useless inconsequence." An innocence, a simplicity that one does not find elsewhere in literature makes the birds and the leaves seem as near to him as they are near to children, and the changes of the seasons great events as before our thoughts had arisen between them and us. At times I wonder if he has it from the literature of Bengal or from religion, and at other times, remembering the birds alighting on his brother's hands, I find pleasure in thinking it hereditary, a mystery that was growing through the centuries like the courtesy of a Tristan or a Pelanore. Indeed, when he is speaking of children, so much a part of himself this quality seems, one is not certain that he is not also speaking of the saints, "They build their houses with sand and they play with empty shells. With withered leaves they weave their boats and smilingly float them on the vast deep. Children have their play on the seashore of worlds. They know not how to swim, they know not how to cast nets. Pearl fishers dive for pearls, merchants sail in their ships, while children gather pebbles and scatter them again. They seek not for hidden treasures, they know not how to cast nets."

W.B. Yeats, September 1912

Thou hast made me endless, such is thy pleasure. This frail vessel thou emptiest again and again, and fillest it ever with fresh life.
This little flute of a reed thou hast carried over hills and dales, and hast breathed through it melodies eternally new.
At the immortal touch of thy hands my little heart loses its limits in joy and gives birth to utterance ineffable.
Thy infinite gifts come to me only on these very small hands of mine. Ages pass, and still thou pourest, and still there is room to fill.

When thou commandest me to sing it seems that my heart would break with pride; and I look to thy face, and tears come to my eyes.
All that is harsh and dissonant in my life melts into one sweet harmony—and my adoration spreads wings like a glad bird on its flight across the sea.
I know thou takest pleasure in my singing. I know that only as a singer I come before thy presence.
I touch by the edge of the far-spreading wing of my song thy feet which I could never aspire to reach.
Drunk with the joy of singing I forget myself and call thee friend who art my lord.

I know not how thou singest, my master! I ever listen in silent amazement.
The light of thy music illumines the world. The life breath of thy music runs from sky to sky. The holy stream of thy music breaks through all stony obstacles and rushes on.
My heart longs to join in thy song, but vainly struggles for a voice. I would speak, but speech breaks not into song, and I cry out baffled. Ah, thou hast made my heart captive in the endless meshes of thy music, my master!

Life of my life, I shall ever try to keep my body pure, knowing that thy living touch is upon all my limbs.
I shall ever try to keep all untruths out from my thoughts, knowing that thou art that truth which has kindled the light of reason in my mind.
I shall ever try to drive all evils away from my heart and keep my love in flower, knowing that thou hast thy seat in the inmost shrine of my heart.

And it shall be my endeavour to reveal thee in my actions, knowing it is thy power gives me strength to act.

I ask for a moment's indulgence to sit by thy side. The works that I have in hand I will finish afterwards.
Away from the sight of thy face my heart knows no rest nor respite, and my work becomes an endless toil in a shoreless sea of toil.
Today the summer has come at my window with its sighs and murmurs; and the bees are plying their minstrelsy at the court of the flowering grove.
Now it is time to sit quiet, face to face with thee, and to sing dedication of life in this silent and overflowing leisure.

Pluck this little flower and take it, delay not! I fear lest it droop and drop into the dust.
I may not find a place in thy garland, but honour it with a touch of pain from thy hand and pluck it. I fear lest the day end before I am aware, and the time of offering go by.
Though its colour be not deep and its smell be faint, use this flower in thy service and pluck it while there is time.

My song has put off her adornments. She has no pride of dress and decoration. Ornaments would mar our union; they would come between thee and me; their jingling would drown thy whispers.
My poet's vanity dies in shame before thy sight. O master poet, I have sat down at thy feet. Only let me make my life simple and straight, like a flute of reed for thee to fill with music.

The child who is decked with prince's robes and who has jewelled chains round his neck loses all pleasure in his play; his dress hampers him at every step.
In fear that it may be frayed, or stained with dust he keeps himself from the world, and is afraid even to move.
Mother, it is no gain, thy bondage of finery, if it keep one shut off from the healthful dust of the earth, if it rob one of the right of entrance to the great fair of common human life.

O Fool, try to carry thyself upon thy own shoulders! O beggar, to come beg at thy own door!
Leave all thy burdens on his hands who can bear all, and never look behind in regret.

Thy desire at once puts out the light from the lamp it touches with its breath. It is unholy—take not thy gifts through its unclean hands. Accept only what is offered by sacred love.

Here is thy footstool and there rest thy feet where live the poorest, and lowliest, and lost.
When I try to bow to thee, my obeisance cannot reach down to the depth where thy feet rest among the poorest, and lowliest, and lost.
Pride can never approach to where thou walkest in the clothes of the humble among the poorest, and lowliest, and lost.
My heart can never find its way to where thou keepest company with the companionless among the poorest, the lowliest, and the lost.

Leave this chanting and singing and telling of beads! Whom dost thou worship in this lonely dark corner of a temple with doors all shut? Open thine eyes and see thy God is not before thee!
He is there where the tiller is tilling the hard ground and where the pathmaker is breaking stones. He is with them in sun and in shower, and his garment is covered with dust. Put off thy holy mantle and even like him come down on the dusty soil!
Deliverance? Where is this deliverance to be found? Our master himself has joyfully taken upon him the bonds of creation; he is bound with us all for ever.
Come out of thy meditations and leave aside thy flowers and incense! What harm is there if thy clothes become tattered and stained? Meet him and stand by him in toil and in sweat of thy brow.

The time that my journey takes is long and the way of it long.
I came out on the chariot of the first gleam of light, and pursued my voyage through the wildernesses of worlds leaving my track on many a star and planet.
It is the most distant course that comes nearest to thyself, and that training is the most intricate which leads to the utter simplicity of a tune.
The traveller has to knock at every alien door to come to his own, and one has to wander through all the outer worlds to reach the innermost shrine at the end.

My eyes strayed far and wide before I shut them and said "Here art thou!"
The question and the cry "Oh, where?" melt into tears of a thousand streams and deluge the world with the flood of the assurance "I am!"

The song that I came to sing remains unsung to this day.
I have spent my days in stringing and in unstringing my instrument.
The time has not come true, the words have not been rightly set; only there is the agony of wishing in my heart.
The blossom has not opened; only the wind is sighing by.
I have not seen his face, nor have I listened to his voice; only I have heard his gentle footsteps from the road before my house.
The livelong day has passed in spreading his seat on the floor; but the lamp has not been lit and I cannot ask him into my house.
I live in the hope of meeting with him; but this meeting is not yet.

My desires are many and my cry is pitiful, but ever didst thou save me by hard refusals; and this strong mercy has been wrought into my life through and through.
Day by day thou art making me worthy of the simple, great gifts that thou gavest to me unasked—this sky and the light, this body and the life and the mind—saving me from perils of overmuch desire.
There are times when I languidly linger and times when I awaken and hurry in search of my goal; but cruelly thou hidest thyself from before me.
Day by day thou art making me worthy of thy full acceptance by refusing me ever and anon, saving me from perils of weak, uncertain desire.

I am here to sing thee songs. In this hall of thine I have a corner seat.
In thy world I have no work to do; my useless life can only break out in tunes without a purpose.
When the hour strikes for thy silent worship at the dark temple of midnight, command me, my master, to stand before thee to sing.

When in the morning air the golden harp is tuned, honour me, commanding my presence.

I have had my invitation to this world's festival, and thus my life has been blessed. My eyes have seen and my ears have heard.
It was my part at this feast to play upon my instrument, and I have done all I could.
Now, I ask, has the time come at last when I may go in and see thy face and offer thee my silent salutation?

I am only waiting for love to give myself up at last into his hands. That is why it is so late and why I have been guilty of such omissions.
They come with their laws and their codes to bind me fast; but I evade them ever, for I am only waiting for love to give myself up at last into his hands.
People blame me and call me heedless; I doubt not they are right in their blame.
The market day is over and work is all done for the busy. Those who came to call me in vain have gone back in anger. I am only waiting for love to give myself up at last into his hands.

Clouds heap upon clouds and it darkens. Ah, love, why dost thou let me wait outside at the door all alone?
In the busy moments of the noontide work I am with the crowd, but on this dark lonely day it is only for thee that I hope.
If thou showest me not thy face, if thou leavest me wholly aside, I know not how I am to pass these long, rainy hours.
I keep gazing on the far-away gloom of the sky, and my heart wanders wailing with the restless wind.

If thou speakest not I will fill my heart with thy silence and endure it. I will keep still and wait like the night with starry vigil and its head bent low with patience.
The morning will surely come, the darkness will vanish, and thy voice pour down in golden streams breaking through the sky.
Then thy words will take wing in songs from every one of my birds" nests, and thy melodies will break forth in flowers in all my forest groves.

On the day when the lotus bloomed, alas, my mind was straying, and I knew it not. My basket was empty and the flower remained unheeded.

Only now and again a sadness fell upon me, and I started up from my dream and felt a sweet trace of a strange fragrance in the south wind.

That vague sweetness made my heart ache with longing and it seemed to me that it was the eager breath of the summer seeking for its completion.

I knew not then that it was so near, that it was mine, and that this perfect sweetness had blossomed in the depth of my own heart.

I must launch out my boat. The languid hours pass by on the shore—Alas for me!

The spring has done its flowering and taken leave. And now with the burden of faded futile flowers I wait and linger.

The waves have become clamorous, and upon the bank in the shady lane the yellow leaves flutter and fall.

What emptiness do you gaze upon! Do you not feel a thrill passing through the air with the notes of the far-away song floating from the other shore?

In the deep shadows of the rainy July, with secret steps, thou walkest, silent as night, eluding all watchers.

Today the morning has closed its eyes, heedless of the insistent calls of the loud east wind, and a thick veil has been drawn over the ever-wakeful blue sky.

The woodlands have hushed their songs, and doors are all shut at every house. Thou art the solitary wayfarer in this deserted street. Oh my only friend, my best beloved, the gates are open in my house—do not pass by like a dream.

Art thou abroad on this stormy night on thy journey of love, my friend? The sky groans like one in despair.

I have no sleep tonight. Ever and again I open my door and look out on the darkness, my friend!

I can see nothing before me. I wonder where lies thy path!

By what dim shore of the ink-black river, by what far edge of the frowning forest, through what mazy depth of gloom art thou threading thy course to come to me, my friend?

If the day is done, if birds sing no more, if the wind has flagged tired, then draw the veil of darkness thick upon me, even as thou hast wrapt the earth with the coverlet of sleep and tenderly closed the petals of the drooping lotus at dusk.

From the traveller, whose sack of provisions is empty before the voyage is ended, whose garment is torn and dustladen, whose strength is exhausted, remove shame and poverty, and renew his life like a flower under the cover of thy kindly night.

In the night of weariness let me give myself up to sleep without struggle, resting my trust upon thee.

Let me not force my flagging spirit into a poor preparation for thy worship.

It is thou who drawest the veil of night upon the tired eyes of the day to renew its sight in a fresher gladness of awakening.

He came and sat by my side but I woke not. What a cursed sleep it was, O miserable me!

He came when the night was still; he had his harp in his hands, and my dreams became resonant with its melodies.

Alas, why are my nights all thus lost? Ah, why do I ever miss his sight whose breath touches my sleep?

Light, oh where is the light? Kindle it with the burning fire of desire!

There is the lamp but never a flicker of a flame—is such thy fate, my heart? Ah, death were better by far for thee!

Misery knocks at thy door, and her message is that thy lord is wakeful, and he calls thee to the love-tryst through the darkness of night.

The sky is overcast with clouds and the rain is ceaseless. I know not what this is that stirs in me—I know not its meaning.

A moment's flash of lightning drags down a deeper gloom on my sight, and my heart gropes for the path to where the music of the night calls me.

Light, oh where is the light! Kindle it with the burning fire of desire! It thunders and the wind rushes screaming through the void. The night is black as a black stone. Let not the hours pass by in the dark. Kindle the lamp of love with thy life.

Obstinate are the trammels, but my heart aches when I try to break them.
Freedom is all I want, but to hope for it I feel ashamed.
I am certain that priceless wealth is in thee, and that thou art my best friend, but I have not the heart to sweep away the tinsel that fills my room.
The shroud that covers me is a shroud of dust and death; I hate it, yet hug it in love.
My debts are large, my failures great, my shame secret and heavy; yet when I come to ask for my good, I quake in fear lest my prayer be granted.

He whom I enclose with my name is weeping in this dungeon. I am ever busy building this wall all around; and as this wall goes up into the sky day by day I lose sight of my true being in its dark shadow.
I take pride in this great wall, and I plaster it with dust and sand lest a least hole should be left in this name; and for all the care I take I lose sight of my true being.

I came out alone on my way to my tryst. But who is this that follows me in the silent dark?
I move aside to avoid his presence but I escape him not.
He makes the dust rise from the earth with his swagger; he adds his loud voice to every word that I utter.
He is my own little self, my lord, he knows no shame; but I am ashamed to come to thy door in his company.

"Prisoner, tell me, who was it that bound you?"
"It was my master," said the prisoner. "I thought I could outdo everybody in the world in wealth and power, and I amassed in my own treasure-house the money due to my king. When sleep overcame me I lay upon the bed that was for my lord, and on waking up I found I was a prisoner in my own treasure-house."
"Prisoner, tell me, who was it that wrought this unbreakable chain?"
"It was I," said the prisoner, "who forged this chain very carefully. I thought my invincible power would hold the world captive, leaving me in a freedom undisturbed. Thus night and day I worked at the chain with huge fires and cruel hard strokes. When at last the work was done and the links were complete and unbreakable, I found that it held me in its grip."

By all means they try to hold me secure who love me in this world. But it is otherwise with thy love which is greater than theirs, and thou keepest me free.

Lest I forget them they never venture to leave me alone. But day passes by after day and thou art not seen.

If I call not thee in my prayers, if I keep not thee in my heart, thy love for me still waits for my love.

When it was day they came into my house and said, "We shall only take the smallest room here."

They said, "We shall help you in the worship of your God and humbly accept only our own share in his grace"; and then they took their seat in a corner and they sat quiet and meek.

But in the darkness of night I find they break into my sacred shrine, strong and turbulent, and snatch with unholy greed the offerings from God's altar.

Let only that little be left of me whereby I may name thee my all.

Let only that little be left of my will whereby I may feel thee on every side, and come to thee in everything, and offer to thee my love every moment.

Let only that little be left of me whereby I may never hide thee.

Let only that little of my fetters be left whereby I am bound with thy will, and thy purpose is carried out in my life—and that is the fetter of thy love.

✧ Hind Swaraj ✧

Mohandas K. Gandhi

British rule in India was, by most colonial standards, relatively efficient and, in the view of the British administrators themselves, benign. Educated Indians resented foreign domination but were at the same time so imbued with British culture as to make it difficult for them to consider using violence against their imperial masters. They were restrained in their criticism of the British until an "extremist" faction of India's nationalist movement appeared in the late nineteenth century. This faction was suppressed, along with a short-lived terrorist outburst after 1905, on the charge of inciting revolution. The situation appeared at an impasse until an Indian leader emerged who was able to show his countrymen a way to drive out the British without violence.

Mohandas K. Gandhi (1869–1948) was born in the native state of Porbandar, in western India. His father and grandfather had served as prime ministers to the native prince of the region. It was decided that Gandhi should pursue law, and he was sent to London in 1888 for his legal studies. During his three years in an alien culture, he became more aware of his Indian roots and was led by his study of the *Bhagavad Gita* to a greater appreciation of the concept of selfless service. Having completed his law degree, he accepted a position in South Africa. Here he was made personally aware that, although Indians were subjects of the same queen as whites, they possessed few of the rights of their fellow-subjects.

Gandhi became the leader and spokesman for the Indian community in South Africa and, from 1893 to 1914, worked fearlessly and effectively to gain his countrymen rights and protection under the law. Influenced in part by the ideas of Leo Tolstoy, he developed the policy he called *satyagraha* (soul-force or truth-force), which included the use of "passive resistance." Generally speaking, *satyagraha* meant that one should neither obey an unjust law nor cooperate in its enforcement, even at the cost of personal punishment. His application of that principle led to his imprisonment, but also it led the British government in South Africa to accord the Indian population of that area a somewhat greater respect.

News of Gandhi's efforts reached India, and when he returned home in 1915, he found himself a popular hero and much sought-after by Indian political leaders. He undertook a year's travel about India to acquaint himself with local conditions and to begin to spread among the masses his philosophy of *satyagraha*. He took pains to identify himself with the Indian people in dress, speech, and way of life, encouraging other Indian leaders to follow his lead. In this way, the Indian educated class began to be drawn away from its dependence on the British.

The Gujarati version of Gandhi's book *Hind Swaraj* was serialized in 1909 in the journal *Indian Opinion*. He reprinted the English version in India in 1921 and 1938, reaffirming his commitment to its position each time. The term Gandhi translated as "home rule" is *swaraj*, literally "self-rule." It had been in the vocabulary of extremist nationalists for years in the sense of Indian independence from British imperialism, and to most leaders of the Indian National Congress, the term implied a British view of self-government: a parliamentary model of liberal democracy. As the following excerpt shows, Gandhi used the term in more than a political sense. It has a psychological connotation, "ruling the self," which he related to traditional Indian virtues of self-control. It also implies economic self-sufficiency. Gandhi thought that all the necessities of life could be met by redistribution of wealth, reducing consumption, and small-scale production. Gandhi dreamed of a united and independent India, with its economy and society centered on the traditional Indian village community, and its national spirit united by a concept of selfless service that would transcend considerations of caste, faith, race, and wealth.

The website http://www.mkgandhi.org contains a wealth of information on Gandhi.

Questions

1. How does Gandhi's definition of "civilization" differ from other definitions?
2. How does he explain India's subjugation to England?
3. Is Gandhi's tactic of passive resistance still viable, or was it only possible in the special conditions of the British Empire in India?

Hind Swaraj

"Hind Swaraj," in *Indian Home Rule by M.K. Gandhi. Being a translation of "Hind Swaraj" (Indian Home Rule), published in the Gujarati columns of* Indian Opinion, *11th and 18th December 1909* (Phoenix, Natal: International Printing Press, 1910), pp. 6–7, 14–15, 19–24, 36–37, 39, 47–50, 52–53, 61, 64

Preface

I have written some chapters on the subject of Indian Home Rule which I venture to place before the readers of *Indian Opinion*. I have written because I could not restrain myself. I have read much, I have pondered much, during the stay, for four months in London, of the Transvaal Indian deputation. I discussed things with as many of my countrymen as I could. I met, too, as many Englishmen as it was possible for me to meet. I consider it my duty now to place before the readers of *Indian Opinion* the conclusions, which appear to me to be final. The Gujarati subscribers of *Indian Opinion* number about 800. I am aware that, for every subscriber, there are at least ten persons who read the paper with zest. Those who cannot read Gujarati have the paper read out to them. Such persons have often questioned me about the condition of India. Similar questions were addressed to me in London. I felt, therefore, that it might not be improper for me to ventilate publicly the views expressed by me in private. . . .

The only motive is to serve my country, to find out the Truth, and to follow it. If, therefore, my views are proved to be wrong, I shall have no hesitation in rejecting them. If they are proved to be right, I would naturally wish, for the sake of the motherland, that others should adopt them.

To make it easy reading, the chapters are written in the form of a dialogue between the reader and the editor.

Reader: I have now learnt what the Congress has done to make India one nation, how the Partition has caused an awakening, and how discontent and unrest have spread through the land. I would now like to know your views on Swaraj. I fear that our interpretation is not the same as yours.

Editor: It is quite possible that we do not attach the same meaning to the term. You and I and all Indians are impatient to obtain Swaraj, but we are certainly not decided as to what it is. To drive the English out of India is a thought heard from many mouths, but it does not seem that many have properly considered why it should be so. I must ask you a question. Do you think that it is necessary to drive away the English, if we get all we want?

Reader: I should ask of them only one thing, that is: "Please leave our country." If, after they have complied with this request, their withdrawal from India means that they are still in India, I should have no objection. Then we would understand that, in their language, the word "gone" is equivalent to "remained."

Editor: Well then, let us suppose that the English have retired. What will you do then?

Reader: That question cannot be answered at this stage. The state after withdrawal will depend largely upon the manner of it. If, as you assume, they retire, it seems to me we shall still keep their constitution and shall carry on the Government. If they simply retire for the asking, we should have an army, etc., ready at hand. We should, therefore, have no difficulty in carrying on the Government.

Editor: You may think so; I do not. But I will not discuss the matter just now. I have to answer your question, and that I can do well by asking you several questions. Why do you want to drive away the English?

Reader: Because India has become impoverished by their Government. They take away our money from year to year. The most important posts are reserved for themselves. We are kept in a state of slavery. They behave insolently towards us and disregard our feelings.

Editor: If they do not take our money away, become gentle, and give us responsible posts, would you still consider their presence to be harmful?

Reader: That question is useless. It is similar to the question whether there is any harm in associating with a tiger if he changes his nature. Such a question is sheer waste of time. When a tiger changes his nature, Englishmen will change theirs. This is not possible, and to believe it to be possible is contrary to human experience. . . . Now will you tell me something of what you have read and thought of this civilization?

Editor: Let us first consider what state of things is described by the word "civilization." Its true test lies in the fact that people living in it make bodily welfare the object of life. We will take some examples. The people of Europe today live in better-built houses than they did a hundred years ago. This is considered an emblem of civilization, and this is also a matter to promote bodily happiness. Formerly, they wore skins, and used spears as their weapons. Now, they wear long trousers, and, for embellishing their bodies, they wear a variety of clothing, and, instead of spears, they carry with them revolvers containing five or more chambers. If people of a certain country, who have hitherto not been in the habit of wearing much clothing, boots, etc., adopt European clothing, they are supposed to have become civilized out of savagery. Formerly in Europe, people ploughed their lands mainly by manual labour. Now, one man can plough a vast tract by means of steam engines and can thus amass great wealth. This is called a sign of civilization. Formerly, only a few men wrote valuable books. Now, anybody writes and prints anything he likes and poisons people's minds. . . . Formerly, men worked in the open air only as much as they liked. Now thousands of workmen meet together and for the sake of maintenance work in factories or mines. Their condition is worse than that of beasts. They are obliged to work, at the risk of their lives, at most dangerous occupations, for the sake of millionaires. Formerly, men were made slaves under physical compulsion. Now they are enslaved by temptation of money and of the luxuries that money can buy. There are now diseases of which people never dreamt before, and an army of doctors is engaged in finding out their cures, and so hospitals have increased. This is a test of civilization. Formerly, special messengers were required and much expense was incurred in order to send letters; today, anyone can abuse his fellow by means of a letter for one penny. True, at the same cost, one can send one's thanks also. Formerly, people had two or three meals consisting of home-made bread and vegetables; now, they require something to eat every two hours so that they have hardly leisure for anything else.

What more need I say? All this you can ascertain from several authoritative books. These are all true tests of civilization. And if anyone speaks to the contrary, know that he is ignorant. This civilization takes note neither of morality nor of religion. Its votaries calmly state that their business is not to teach religion. Some even consider it to be a superstitious growth. Others put on the cloak of religion, and prate about morality. But, after twenty years' experience, I have come to the conclusion that immorality is often taught in the name of morality. Even a child can understand that in all I have described above there can be no inducement to morality. Civilization seeks to increase bodily comforts, and it fails miserably even in doing so.

This civilization is irreligion, and it has taken such a hold on the people in Europe that those who are in it appear to be half mad. They lack real physical strength or courage. They keep up their energy by intoxication. They can hardly be happy in solitude. Women, who should be the queens of households, wander in the streets or they slave away in factories. For the sake of a pittance, half a million women in England alone are labouring under trying circumstances in factories or similar institutions. This awful fact is one of the causes of the daily growing suffragette movement.

This civilization is such that one has only to be patient and it will be self-destroyed. According to the teaching of Mahomed this would be considered a Satanic Civilization. Hinduism calls it the Black Age. I cannot give you an adequate conception of it. It is eating into the vitals of the English nation. It must be shunned. Parliaments are really emblems of slavery. If you will sufficiently think over this, you will entertain the same opinion and cease to blame the English. They rather deserve our sympathy. They are a shrewd nation and I therefore believe that they will cast off the evil. They are enterprising and industrious, and their mode of thought is not inherently immoral. Neither are they bad at heart. I therefore respect them. Civilization is not an incurable disease, but it should never be forgotten that the English people are at present afflicted by it.

The English have not taken India; we have given it to them. They are not in India because of their strength, but because we keep them. Let us now see whether these propositions can be sustained. They came to our country originally for purposes of trade. Recall the Company Bahadur ["Warrior Company, the name the British gave the East India Company]. Who made it Bahadur? They had not the slightest intention at the time of establishing a kingdom. Who assisted the Company's officers? Who was tempted at the sight of their silver? Who bought their goods? History testifies that we did all this. In order to become rich all at once we welcomed the Company's officers with open arms. We assisted them. If I am in the habit of drinking *bhang* [marijuana] and a seller thereof sells it to me, am I to blame him or myself? By blaming the seller, shall I be able to avoid the habit? And, if a particular retailer is driven away, will not another take his place? A true servant of India will have to go to the root of the matter.

Editor: The causes that gave them India enable them to retain it. Some Englishmen state that they took and they hold India by the sword. Both these statements are wrong. The sword is entirely useless for holding India. We alone keep them. Napoleon is said to have described the English as a nation of shop-keepers. It is a fitting description. They hold whatever dominions they have for the sake of their commerce. Their army and their navy are intended to protect it. . . . Many problems can be solved by remembering that money is their God. Then it follows that we keep the English in India for our base self-interest. We like their commerce; they please us by their subtle methods and get what they want from us. To blame them for this is to perpetuate their power. We further strengthen their hold by quarrelling amongst ourselves. If you accept the above statements, it is proved that the English entered India for the purposes of trade. They remain in it for the same purpose and we help them to do so. Their arms and ammunition are perfectly useless.

Reader: I now understand why the English hold India. I should like to know your views about the condition of our country.

Editor: It is a sad condition. In thinking of it my eyes water and my throat gets parched. I have grave doubts whether I shall be able sufficiently to explain what is in my heart. It is my deliberate opinion that India is being ground down, not under the English heel, but under that of modern civilization. It is groaning under the monster's terrible weight. There is yet time to escape it, but every day makes it more and more difficult. Religion is dear to me and my first complaint is that India is becoming irreligious. Here I am not thinking of the Hindu or the Mahomedan or the Zoroastrian religion but of that religion which underlies all religions. We are turning away from God.

Reader: How so?

Editor: There is a charge laid against us that we are a lazy people and that Europeans are industrious and enterprising. We have accepted the charge and we therefore wish to change our condition. Hinduism, Islam, Zoroastrianism, Christianity and all other religions teach that we should remain passive about worldly pursuits and active about godly pursuits, that we should set a limit to our worldly ambition and that our religious ambition should be illimitable. Our activity should be directed into the latter channel.

Reader: You have denounced railways, lawyers and doctors. I can see that you will discard all machinery. What, then, is civilization?

Editor: The answer to that question is not difficult. I believe that the civilization India has evolved is not to be beaten in the world. Nothing can equal the seeds sown by our ancestors. Rome went, Greece shared the same fate; the might of the Pharaohs was broken; Japan has become westernized; of China nothing can be said; but India is still, somehow or other, sound at the foundation. The people of Europe learn their lessons from the writings of the men of Greece or Rome, which exist no longer in their former glory. In trying to learn from them, the Europeans imagine that they will avoid the mistakes of Greece and Rome. Such is their pitiable condition. In the midst of all this India remains immovable and that is her glory. It is a charge against India that her people are so uncivilized, ignorant and stolid, that it is not possible to induce them to adopt any changes. It is a charge really against our merit. What we have tested and found true on the anvil of experience, we dare not change. Many thrust their advice upon India, and she remains steady. This is her beauty: it is the sheet anchor of our hope.

Civilization is that mode of conduct which points out to man the path of duty. Performance of duty and observance of morality are convertible terms. To observe morality is to attain mastery over our mind and our passions. So doing, we know ourselves. The Gujarati equivalent for civilization means "good conduct."

If this definition be correct, then India, as so many writers have shown, has nothing to learn from anybody else, and this is as it should be.

Reader: If Indian civilization is, as you say, the best of all, how do you account for India's slavery?

Editor: This civilization is unquestionably the best, but it is to be observed that all civilizations have been on their trial. That civilization which is permanent outlives it. Because the sons of India were found wanting, its civilization has been placed in jeopardy. But its strength is to be seen in its ability to survive the shock. Moreover, the whole of India is not touched. Those alone who have been affected by Western civilization have become enslaved. We measure the universe by our own miserable foot-rule. When we are slaves, we think that the whole universe is enslaved. Because we are in an abject condition, we think that the whole of India is in that condition. As a matter of fact, it is not so, yet it is as well to impute our slavery to the whole of India. But if we bear in mind the above fact, we can see that if we become free, India is free. And in this thought you have a definition of Swaraj. It is Swaraj when we learn to rule ourselves. It is, therefore, in the palm of our hands. Do not consider this Swaraj to be like a dream. There is no idea of sitting still. The Swaraj that I wish to picture is such that, after we have once realized it, we shall endeavour to the end of our life-time to persuade others to do likewise. But such Swaraj has to be experienced, by each one for himself. One drowning man will never save another. Slaves ourselves, it would be a mere pretension to think of freeing others. Now you will have seen that it is not necessary for us to have as our goal the expulsion of the English. If the English become Indianized, we can accommodate them. If they wish to remain in India along with their civilization, there is no room for them. It lies with us to bring about such a state of things.

Editor: Passive resistance is a method of securing rights by personal suffering; it is the reverse of resistance by arms. When I refuse to do a thing that is repugnant to my conscience, I use soul-force [*satyagraha*]. For instance, the Government of the day has passed a law which is applicable to me. I do not like it. If by using violence I force the Government to repeal the law, I am employing what may be termed body-force. If I do not obey the law and accept the penalty for its breach, I use soul-force. It involves sacrifice of self.

Everybody admits that sacrifice of self is infinitely superior to sacrifice of others. Moreover, if this kind of force is used in a cause that is unjust, only the person using it suffers. He does not make others suffer for his mistakes. Men have before now done many things which were subsequently found to have been wrong. No man can claim that he is absolutely in the right or that a particular thing is wrong because he thinks so, but it is wrong for him so long as that is his deliberate judgment. It is therefore meet that he should not do that which he knows to be wrong, and suffer the consequence whatever it may be. This is the key to the use of soul-force.

Reader: From what you say I deduce that passive resistance is a splendid weapon of the weak, but that when they are strong they may take up arms.

Editor: This is gross ignorance. Passive resistance, that is, soul-force, is matchless. It is superior to the force of arms. How, then, can it be considered only a weapon of the weak? Physical-force men are strangers to the courage that is requisite in a passive resister. Do you believe that a coward can ever disobey a law that he dislikes? Extremists are considered to be advocates of brute force. Why do they, then, talk about obeying laws? I do not blame them. They can say nothing else. When they succeed in driving out the English and they themselves become governors, they will want you and me to obey their laws. And that is a fitting thing for their constitution. But a passive resister will say he will not obey a law that is against his conscience, even though he may be blown to pieces at the mouth of a cannon. . . . It is difficult to become a passive resister unless the body is trained. As a rule, the mind, residing in a body that has become weakened by pampering, is also weak, and where there is no strength of mind there can be no strength of soul. We shall have to improve our physique by getting rid of infant marriages and luxurious living. If I were to ask a man with a shattered body to face a cannon's mouth, I should make a laughing-stock of myself.

Reader: From what you say, then, it would appear that it is not a small thing to become a passive resister, and, if that is so, I should like you to explain how a man may become one.

Editor: To become a passive resister is easy enough but it is also equally difficult. I have known a lad of fourteen years become a passive resister; I have known also sick people do likewise; and I have also known physically strong and otherwise happy people unable to take up passive resistance. After a great deal of experience it seems to me that those who want to become passive resisters for the service of the country have to observe perfect chastity, adopt poverty, follow truth, and cultivate fearlessness.

Chastity is one of the great disciplines without which the mind cannot attain requisite firmness. A man who is unchaste loses stamina, becomes emasculated and cowardly. He whose mind is given over to animal passions is not capable of any great effort. This can be proved by innumerable instances. What, then, is a married person to do is the question that arises naturally; and yet it need not. When a husband and wife gratify the passions, it is no less an animal indulgence on that account. Such an indulgence, except for perpetuating the race, is strictly prohibited. But a passive resister has to avoid even that very limited indulgence because he can have no desire for progeny. A married man, therefore, can observe perfect chastity. This subject is not capable of being treated at greater length. Several questions arise: How is one to carry one's wife with one, what are her rights, and other similar questions. Yet those who wish to take part in a great work are bound to solve these puzzles.

Just as there is necessity for chastity, so is there for poverty. Pecuniary ambition and passive resistance cannot well go together. Those who have money are not expected to throw it away, but they are expected to be indifferent about it. They must be prepared to lose every penny rather than give up passive resistance.

Passive resistance has been described in the course of our discussion as truth-force. Truth, therefore, has necessarily to be followed and that at any cost. In this connection, academic questions such as whether a man may not lie in order to save a life, etc., arise, but these questions occur only to those who wish to justify lying. Those who want to follow truth every time are not placed in such a quandary; and if they are, they are still saved from a false position.

Passive resistance cannot proceed a step without fearlessness. Those alone can follow the path of passive resistance who are free from fear, whether as to their possessions, false honour, their relatives, the government, bodily injuries or death.

Reader: What, then, would you say to the English?

Editor: To them I would respectfully say: "I admit you are my rulers. It is not necessary to debate the question whether you hold India by the sword or by my consent. I have no objection to your remaining in my country, but although you are the rulers, you will have to remain as servants of the people. It is not we who have to do as you wish, but it is you who have to do as we wish. You may keep the riches that you have drained away from this land, but you may not drain riches henceforth. Your function will be, if you so wish, to police India; you must abandon the idea of deriving any commercial benefit from us. We hold the civilization that you support to be the reverse of civilization. We consider our civilization to be far superior to yours. If you realize this truth, it will be to your advantage and, if you do not, according to your own proverb, you should only live in our country in the same manner as we do. You must not do anything that is contrary to our religions. It is your duty as rulers that for the sake of the Hindus you should eschew beef, and for the sake of Mahomedans you should avoid bacon and ham. We have hitherto said nothing because we have been cowed down, but you need not consider that you have not hurt our feelings by your conduct. We are not expressing our sentiments either through base selfishness or fear, but because it is our duty now to speak out boldly. We consider your schools and law courts to be useless. We want our own ancient schools and courts to be restored. The common language of India is not English but Hindi. You should, therefore, learn it. We can hold communication with you only in our national language.

Let each do his duty. If I do my duty, that is, serve myself, I shall be able to serve others. Before I leave you, I will take the liberty of repeating:

1. Real home-rule is self-rule or self-control.
2. The way to it is passive resistance: that is soul-force or love-force.
3. In order to exert this force, Swadeshi [domestic production] in every sense is necessary.
4. What we want to do should be done, not because we object to the English or because we want to retaliate but because it is our duty to do so. Thus, supposing that the English remove the salt-tax, restore our money, give the highest posts to Indians, withdraw the English troops, we shall certainly not use their machine-made goods, nor use the English language, nor many of their industries. It is worth noting that these things are, in their nature, harmful, hence we do not want them. I bear no enmity towards the English but I do towards their civilization.

In my opinion, we have used the term "Swaraj" without understanding its real significance. I have endeavoured to explain it as I understand it, and my conscience testifies that my life henceforth is dedicated to its attainment.

✧ Muna and Madan ✧

Lakshmiprasad Devkota

Poetry is the richest genre of twentieth-century Nepali literature. It is diverse and sophisticated, owing much to the accomplishments of three great writers all born near the beginning of the twentieth-century. Lekhnath Paudyal, Balkrishna Sama, and Lakshmiprasad Devkota were the unquestioned founders of Nepali poetry, but it was the genius of Devkota that stands out above the others. In the relatively short span of twenty-five years Devkota produced more than forty books, including plays, stories, essays, translations from world literature, and a novel. His work provided the inspiration for many later Nepali writers.

Born into a Brahman family in Kathmandu in 1909, Devkota received his B.A. in 1930. Married at sixteen years of age, he became a father at nineteen and for most of his life struggled to support his family, usually by teaching. He often complained bitterly that it was impossible to earn a living from writing alone. A prey to deep depressions, Devkota was confined to a hospital in 1939 and was almost suicidal after the death of his son in 1952. His life was a series of financial problems and personal sorrows, but through them all shone a personality of humor, warmth, and deep humanity.

His earliest poems reveal the powerful influence of English Romantic verse. In particular, he was deeply influenced by the writings of Wordsworth, Shelley, Byron, and Keats. Soon, however, Devkota began to spice his poetry with a flavor that was essentially Nepali. The publication of the short epic poem *Muna and Madan* in 1936 marked a significant moment in this development. The poem is based on an old Newar folktale, and much of its charm stems from its simple language and musical meter. He broke new ground by becoming the first Nepali poet to employ the *jhyaure* meter of the folk song, despised by earlier poets as coarse and improper for serious poetry.

In *Muna and Madan*, Devkota describes the horrible economic conditions of Nepal through the characters of two young peasants. Madan, a merchant, decides to travel to Tibet to make his fortune. He intends to spend only a few weeks in the Tibetan city of Lhasa and then return to Kathmandu to grant his aging mother her final wishes. Muna, his wife, is sure that he will never return and implores him to stay. Madan ignores her pleas. Upon arriving in Lhasa, he is captivated by the city's beauty. Suddenly realizing that he has lingered too long in Tibet, he departs for home; however, he falls ill with cholera on the way. In Kathmandu, a suitor tells Muna that her husband has perished. But, in truth, a Tibetan rescues Madan and nurses him back to health. By the time Madan returns home, his mother and wife have died, one of old age and the other of a broken heart. Madan decides that he will follow them and he also dies at the end of the poem.

Muna and Madan was Devkota's most beloved composition: on his deathbed he made the remark that even though all his works might perish after his demise, *Muna and Madan* should be saved. The poem has become the most popular work in the whole of Nepali literature and is still taught in all government schools. Following the success of *Muna and Madan* in 1936, Devkota continued to write prolifically until his death in 1959; in fact, he continued to write within hours of his demise.

Questions

1. According to *Manu and Madan*, on what grounds should a person be judged? How would you judge Madan's behavior?
2. Devkota's writings exhibit a strong belief in the goodness of humble people. Are there examples of this belief in the poem?
3. Life, death, and the afterlife are universal questions that frequent the thoughts of all civilizations. What is the importance of an afterlife in this poem?

Muna and Madan

Michael James Hutt, trans. and ed.,
Himalayan Voices: An Introduction to Modern Nepali Literature
(Berkeley: University of California Press, 1991), pp. 46–51

Muna Pleads with Madan

Madan
I have only my mother, my one lamp of good auspice,
do not desert her, do not make her an orphan,
she has endured nigh sixty winters,
let her take comfort from your moonlight face.
Muna
Shame! For your love of your mother
could not hold you here,
not even your love for your mother!
Her hair is white and hoary with age,
her body is weak and fragile.
You go now as a merchant
to a strange and savage land,
what's to be gained, leave us for Lhasa?
Purses of gold
are like the dirt on your hands,
what can be done with wealth?
Better to eat only nettles and greens
with happiness in your heart.

Madan Goes to Tibet

Hill and mountains, steep and sheer,
rivers to ford by the thousand:
the road to Tibet, deserted and bare,
rocks and earth and poison drizzle,
full of mists and laden with rain,
the wandering wind as cold as ice.

Monks with heads round and shaven,
temples and cremation pillars,
hands and feet grow numb on the road
and are later revived by the fire,

wet leafy boughs make the finest quilts
when the teeth are ringing with cold,
even when boiled, it's inedible:
the rawest, roughest rice.

At last, roofs of gold
grace the evening view:
at the Potala's food, on the valley's edge,
Lhasa herself was smiling,
like a mountain the Potala touched the sky
a filigreed mountain of copper and gold.

The travelers saw the golden roof
of the Dalai Lama's vast palace,
where golden Buddhas hid behind yak-hair awnings,
snowcapped peaks, waters cool,
the leaves so green, mimosa flowers
blooming white on budding trees.

Muna in her Solitude

Muna alone, as beautiful as the flowering lotus,
like moonlight touching the clouds' silver shore,
her gentle lips smile, a shower of pearls,
but she wilts like a flower as winter draws near,
and soon her tears rain down.

Wiping wide eyes, she tends Madan's mother,
but when she sleeps in her lonely room
her pillow is soaked by a thousand cares.

She hides her sorrow in her heart,
concealing it in silence,
like a bird which hides with its wing
the arrow which pierces its heart.
She is only bright by the flickering lamp
when the day draws to its close.

A wilting flower's beauty grows
while Autumn is approaching,
when the clouds' dark edges are silver
and the moon shines ever brighter.

Sadness glares in her heart,
recalling his face at their parting,
wintry tears fall on the flower,
starlight, the night's tears
drip down onto the earth.

A rose grows from the sweetest roots,
but roots are consumed by worms;
the bud which blooms in the city
is the prey of evil men;
pure water is sullied
by dirt from a human hand;
men sow thorns in the paths of men.

Most lovely our Muna at her window,
a city rascal saw her, a fallen fairy,
making a lamp for goddess Bhavani,
oblivious to all.
He saw the tender lobes of her ears,
saw her hair in disarray,
and with this heavenly vision
he rose like a madman and staggered away.

You see the rose is beautiful,
but brother do not touch it!
You look with desire, entranced,
but be not like a savage!
The things of Creation are precious gems,
a flower contains the laughter of God,
do not kill it with your touch!

Madan Tarries in Lhasa

Six months had passed, then seven,
suddenly Madan was startled,
remembering his Muna, his mother:
a wave of water rushed through his heart.

A dove flew over the city,
it crossed the river near the ford,
Madan's mind took wing, flew home,
as he sat he imagined returning,

and Muna's eyes were wide with sorrow,
her wide almond eyes.

"Dong" rang the monastery bell,
the clouds all gathered together,
mountain shadows grew long with evening.
Chilled by the wind in sad meditation,
Madan rose up, saw the moon wrapped in wool,
his mother, his Muna, danced in his eyes,
it became clear to him that night,
his pillow was wet with tears.

His heart oppressed by the reddening sky,
he packed his purses of gold away,
he gathered up his bags of musk,
then took his leave of Lhasa,
calling out to the Lord.

Madan Falls Sick on His Journey Home

Here in the pitiless hills and forests,
the stars, the whole world seemed cruel,
he turned over slowly to moan in the grass . . .
some stranger approached, a torch in his hand,
a robber, a ghost, a bad forest spirit?
Should he hope or should he fear?
His breath hung suspended, but in an instant
the torch was beside him before he knew.

A Tibetan looks to see who is weeping,
he seeks the sick man there,
"Your friends were worthless, but my house is near,
you will not die, I shall carry you home."

Poor Madan falls at his feet,
"At home, I've my white-haired mother
and my wife who shines like a lamp,
save me now and the Lord will see,
he who helps his fellow man
cannot help but go to heaven.
This son of a Chetri touches your feet,
but he touches them not with contempt,

a man must be judged by the size of his heart,
not by his name of his caste."

Madan Departs for Nepal

Far away lies shining Nepal,
where cocks are crowing to summon the light,
as morning opens to smile down from the mountains.
The city of Nepal wears a garland of blue hills,
with trees like earrings on the valley peaks,
the eastern ridges bear rosy clouds,
the fields are bright and dappled with shadows,
water falls like milk from distant hills.

Madan recalls the carved windows and doors,
the *pipal* tree loud in the rising sun,
the little house where Muna sits,
his Muna, his mother, the world of his heart.

"Your kindness has been unbounded,
for you restored my life to me,
a deed I cannot repay.
Two purses of gold I have buried,
now one is mine, the other is yours,
take it and bid me farewell,
I must depart for my home,
as I go forth I remember your charity."

The Tibetan protests,
"What can I do with this yellow gold?
Does gold grow up if you plant it?
You are kind, but we have no use for it,
here are my children, left by their mother,
what use is gold, is wealth,
when Fate has plucked her away?
These children cannot eat gold,
these children do not wear trinkets,
and my wife is above the sky,
the clouds are her only jewels."

The Passing of Madan's Mother

No tears in her eyes now, pervaded by peace,
day's final radiance in pale evening waters,
mainstay of her life, her bar against death: her son far away,
she thinks she sees him, wishfully thinking,
hot with fever, her thin hand is burning
as it lovingly clasps her daughter-in-law's hand.

"My time is near, I must cross to the other world,
no point in weeping, wife of my son.
This is everyone's road, little one,
the road of rich and poor,
this clay turns to clay
and is lost on the shores of sorrow,
and this you must bear:
be not trapped by the snares of grief,
practice devotion which illumines the final path.
I have seen the world's flower garden blooming and wilting,
and in my sorrow, daughter, I have recognized the Lord;
the seeds sown on earth bear fruit in heaven,
my deeds I take with me, but what goes with me, in truth?
The wealth you acquire in this dream
is in your hands when you awake."

Madan Learns of Muna's Death

"My poor brother," says Madan's sister,
"wipe your tears with the edge of my shawl,
be patient, my brother, do not act in this way,
know that we all must go at last,
just a few short days for this sinful body, this dirty pride,
in the end the wind scatters them, a handful of ash,
the flower of the flesh withers away
and mixes once more with the soil,
but a second flower blooms beyond this earth
to sway forever in a heavenly breeze.
We were born to bear sorrow,
to be made pure by suffering;
on our way to the heavenly mansions
we bathe in rivers of tears."

"Do not look down," cries Madan,
"Muna, I come to join you now,
you left a diamond of love here below,
and I shall return it to you . . .
I am veiled, obstructed by the curtain of Death,
I shall not weep, I shall set out tomorrow,
lift the curtain, oh Fate,
quickly now, and you will be blessed."

The clouds parted, a lovely moon smiled down,
it peered with the stars through the clear glass pane,
the clouds drew together, Madan slept forever,
next day, the sun rose in the clearest of skies.

✧ What Is India? ✧

Jawaharlal Nehru

The last British viceroy, Lord Louis Mountbatten, decided to grant India independence within the British Commonwealth of Nations on August 15, 1947, but adopted the demand of Muslim leaders, concentrated in the west and east, that the land be partitioned into two nations, India and Pakistan. Boundaries were to be settled by arbitration on the basis of population, at least in theory. Hundreds of Indian princes, some governing territories larger than many nation-states, could not be dealt with in such summary fashion, but they were forced to choose within which of the new states they wished their lands to be included. It was difficult for the governments of the newly independent and separate states of Pakistan and India to adjust to a situation that many dedicated Indian leaders, including Gandhi, had prayed would never occur.

A constituent assembly, elected in 1946 to draft a constitution for an undivided India, had formulated the document under which India lives today. It was progressive and modern, embodying all the liberal democratic aspirations of the Indian National Congress and reflecting in particular the viewpoint of Jawaharlal Nehru, head of an interim government and soon to become the first prime minister of India.

Gandhi had envisioned a decentralized state based on the fundamental social, political, and economic unit of the traditional Indian village; he warned that, within a centralized state, the mutual distrust of Muslims and Hindus would surely lead to conflict. Both his idealism and his political realism were ignored as many Indian leaders began to dream of the power that they thought could come only with centralization and nationalism. Many of those dedicated people who still followed Gandhi's leadership and relied on his judgment left the government.

Some Indian National Congress leaders, who feared the capitalism that had led Britain to dominate and exploit India for so long, proposed a more socialist constitution with strong measures against official corruption. Although some of these proposals were eventually adopted by Prime Minister Indira Gandhi, Nehru tried at the time to maintain a delicate balance between socialists and communists on the left and Hindu revivalists on the right. The latter won few concessions in the constitution except for minor policies such as protection of cows, regarded as sacred by the Hindus. Nevertheless, Hindus remained politically active and have gained power as time has passed. Currently some Hindu leaders believe that India should promote and protect the religion and culture of the majority.

India had several distinct and conflicting visions of its economic future at the time of independence. Besides Nehru's democratic socialist concept, a more radical socialist view, and Gandhi's ideas of rural self-sufficiency, there was a liberal capitalist vision. Indians debated the many issues involved with these conflicting economic philosophies: the roles of Gandhian village and cottage industries, which were not important to Nehru but were central to Gandhi's followers; the instruments through which the government would guide and control the economy; the possible nationalization of private enterprises; the role of state enterprises; the future of foreign capital; and many others.

Like Nehru, the capitalists wanted to build a strong, centralized industrial state to defend the nation and to raise the standard of living of the Indian people. Nehru, however, distrusted capitalists, thought capitalism was outmoded, and was not convinced that capitalism would lead to social justice or improve the lot of most of the Indian population. Feeling that such progress could be accomplished only under governmental direction, he wanted not only centralized planning but also governmental ownership of industry. In those cases where business was privately owned, such as where foreign capital investment was involved, Nehru felt that tight governmental control and regulation were necessary. Other leaders distrusted the government and wanted to strengthen the private sector.

While Prime Minister Nehru agreed to a larger role for private industry, partly to reassure foreign investors, who had been a large part of the British colonial economy and constituted a legacy to the new nation.

The first two five-year plans established by the Indian government were based on mixed private and government ownership of industry, and this approach has remained the basic developmental strategy for the government of India ever since. Indian private enterprise was protected from foreign competition and cottage industries were protected from industrial competition.

In 1959, against a background of Muslim-Hindu slaughters and cruel mass migrations of people from one new nation to the other, the wrenching assassination of Gandhi in 1949, and the bitter controversies through which the Indian leaders finally hammered out a national policy, Prime Minister Jawaharlal Nehru looked at the India he was helping to build and attempted to place the birth-pangs of the new nation within the context of the long history of Indian civilization. Reflecting on his administration's emphasis on economic, industrial, and technological growth, he realized that India could drift into a materialism that would be a betrayal of the inspiration of Gandhi and constitute a break with a long and rich Indian tradition. Harmonizing that heritage with the driving economic and technological forces of the modern world was India's challenge for the future.

Questions

1. In light of what you have read about India, how accurate is Nehru's review of Indian history?
2. How does Nehru's attitude toward Marxism and socialism differ from typical American attitudes?
3. Does Nehru seem realistic or unrealistic in his hope for the reconciliation of Indian tradition on one hand and science and technology on the other?
4. Does India seem to have realized Nehru's hopes in the past three decades?

What Is India?

Jawaharlal Nehru, "Synthesis Is Our Tradition,"
in Sarvepalli Gopal, ed., *Jawaharlal Nehru: An Anthology*
(Oxford: Oxford University Press, 1980), pp. 225–230

To endeavor to understand and describe the India of today would be the task of a brave man. To describe tomorrow's India would verge on rashness.

What is India? That is a question which has come back again and again to my mind. The early beginnings of our history filled me with wonder. It was the past of a virile and vigorous race with a questing spirit and an urge for free inquiry and, even in its earliest known period, giving evidence of a mature and tolerant civilization. Accepting life and its joys and burdens, it was ever searching for the ultimate and the universal. It built up a magnificent language, Sanskrit, and through this language, its arts and architecture, it sent its vibrant message to far countries. It produced the Upanishads, the Gita and the Buddha.

Hardly any language in the world has probably played that vital part in the history of a race which Sanskrit has. It was not only the vehicle of the highest thought and some of the finest literature, but it became the uniting bond for India, in spite of its political division. The Ramayana and the Mahabharata were woven into the texture of millions of lives in every generation for thousands of years. I have often wondered, if our race forgot the Buddha, the Upanishads and the great epics, what then will it be like! It would be uprooted and would lose the basic characteristics which have clung to it and given it distinction throughout these long ages. India would cease to be India.

Gradually deterioration set in. Thought lost its freshness and became stale, and the vitality and exuberance of youth gave place to crabbed age. Instead of the spirit of adventure there came lifeless routine, and the broad and exciting vision of the world was cabined and confined and lost in caste divisions, narrow social customs and ceremonials. Even so, India was vital enough to absorb the streams of people that flowed into her mighty ocean of humanity and she never quite forgot the thoughts that had stirred her in the days of her youthful vigor.

Subsequently, India was powerfully influenced by the coming of Islam and Muslim invasions. Western colonial powers followed, bringing a new type of domination and a new colonialism and, at the same time, the impact of fresh ideas and of the industrial civilization that was growing up in Europe. This period culminated, after a long struggle, in independence and now we face the future with all this burden of the past upon us and the confused dreams and stirrings of the future that we seek to build.

We have all these ages represented in us and in our country today. We have the growth of nuclear science and atomic energy in India, and we also have the cowdung age.

In the tumult and confusion of our time, we stand facing both ways, forward to the future and backwards to the past, being pulled in both directions. How can we resolve this conflict and evolve a structure for living which fulfils our material needs and, at the same time, sustains our mind and spirit? What new ideals or old ideals varied and adapted to the new world can we place before our people, and how can we galvanize the people into wakefulness and action?

For the present, in India we are rightly absorbed in the Five-Year Plans and in a tremendous effort to raise our people's living standards. Economic progress is essential and a prerequisite for any other type of advance. But a doubt creeps into our minds. Is this by itself enough or is something else to be added on to it? The Welfare State is a worthwhile ideal, but it may well be rather drab. The examples of states which have achieved that objective bring out new problems and difficulties, which are not solved by material advance alone or by a mechanical civilization. Whether religion is necessary or not, a certain faith in a worthwhile ideal is essential to give substance to our lives and to hold us together.

Change is essential but continuity is also necessary. The future has to be built on the foundations laid in the past and in the present. To deny the past and break with it completely is to uproot ourselves and, sapless, dry up. It was the virtue of Gandhiji to keep his feet firmly planted in the rich traditions of our race and our soil and, at the same time, to function on the revolutionary plane. Above all, he laid stress on truth and peaceful means. Thus he built on old foundations, and at the same time, oriented the structure towards the future.

When Islam came to India in the form of political conquest it brought conflict. It had a twofold effect. On the one hand, it encouraged the tendency of Hindu society to shrink still further within its shell; on the other, it brought a breath of fresh air and fresh ideals, and thus had a certain rejuvenating influence. Hindu society had become a closed system. The Muslims who came from outside brought their own closed system with them. Hence the great problem that faced India during the medieval period was how these two closed systems, each with its strong roots, could develop a healthy relationship. Wise rulers like Akbar and others realized that the only hope for the future lay in some kind of harmony being established.

The philosophy and the world outlook of the old Hindus was amazingly tolerant; and yet they had divided themselves up into numerous separate caste groups and hierarchies. The Muslims had to face a new problem, namely how to live with others as equals. In other countries where they had gone, their success was so great that this problem did not really arise. They came into conflict with Christendom and through hundreds of years the problem was never solved. In India, slowly a synthesis was developed. But before this could be completed, other influences came into play.

The new liberal thought of the West and industrial processes began to affect the mind and life of India. A new nationalism developed, which was inevitably against colonialism and sought independence, and yet which was being progressively affected by the new industrial civilization as well as the language, literature and ways of the West.

Rammohun Roy came, seeking some kind of a synthesis between old India and modem trends. Vivekananda brought back something of the vigour of old Indian thought and dressed it in a modern garb. Political and cultural movements grew up and culminated in Gandhiji and Rabindranath Tagore.

In Europe there had been a fierce conflict between science and traditional religion, and the cosmology of Christianity did not fit in at all with scientific theories. Science did not produce that sense of conflict in India and Indian philosophy could easily accept it without doing any vital injury to its basic conceptions.

In India, as elsewhere, two forces developed—the growth of nationalism and the urge for social justice. Socialism and Marxism became the symbol of this urge for social justice and, apart from their scientific content, had a tremendous emotional appeal for the masses.

Living is a continual adjustment to changing conditions. The rapidity of technological change in the last half century has made the necessity of social change greater than ever, and there is a continual maladjustment. The advance of science and technology makes it definitely possible to solve most of the economic problems of the world and, in particular, to provide the primary necessities of life to everyone all over the world. The methods adopted will have to depend upon the background and cultural development of a country or a community.

Internationally, the major question today is that of world peace. The only course open is for us to accept the world as it is and develop toleration for each other. It should be open to each country to develop in its own way, learning from others, and not being imposed on by them.

Essentially, this calls for a new mental approach. The Panch-sheel, or the Five Principles, offer that approach.

There are conflicts within a nation. In a democratic apparatus with adult suffrage, those conflicts can be solved by normal constitutional methods.

In India we have had most distressing spectacles of conflict based on provincialism or linguism. In the main, it is conflict of class interests that poses problems today, and in such cases vested interests are not easy to displace. Yet we have seen in India powerful vested interests like those of the old princes and of the big jagirdars, talukdars and zamindars [all local controller of land] being removed by peaceful methods, even though that meant a break-up of a well-established system which favoured a privileged few. While, therefore, we must recognize that there is class conflict, there is no reason why we should not deal with it through these peaceful methods. They will only succeed, however, if we have a proper objective in view clearly understood by the people.

We have deliberately laid down as our objective a socialist pattern of society. Personally I think that the acquisitive society, which is the base of capitalism, is no longer suited to the present age. We have to evolve a higher order more in keeping with modern trends and conditions and involving not so much competition but much greater cooperation. We have accepted socialism as our goal not only because it seems to us right and beneficial but because there is no other way for the solution of our economic problems. It is sometimes said that rapid progress cannot take place by peaceful and democratic methods. I do not accept this proposition. Indeed, in India today any attempt to discard democratic methods would lead to disruption and would thus put an end to any immediate prospect of progress.

The mighty task that we have undertaken demands the fullest cooperation from the masses of our people. The change we seek necessitates burdens on our people, even on those who can least bear them; unless they realize that they are partners in the building of a society which will bring them benefits, they will not accept these burdens or give their full cooperation.

Whether in land or industry, or in the governmental apparatus, institutional changes become necessary from time to time as functions change. A new set of values will replace those that have governed the old acquisitive society based on the profit motive. The problem before us is ultimately to change the thinking and activities of hundreds of millions of people, and to do this democratically by their consent.

India today presents a very mixed picture of hope and anguish, of remarkable advances and at the same time of inertia, of a new spirit and also the dead hand of the past and of privilege, of an overall and growing unity and many disruptive tendencies. Withal there is a great vitality and a ferment in people's minds and activities.

It is a remarkable thing that a country and a people rooted in the remote past, who have shown so much resistance to change in the past, should now be marching forward rapidly and with resolute steps.

What will emerge from the labour and the tumults of the present generation? I cannot say what will tomorrow's India be like. I can only express my hopes and wishes. I want India to advance on the material plane—to fulfil her Five-Year Plans to raise the standards of living of her vast population; I want the narrow conflicts of today in the name of religion or caste, language or province, to cease, and a classless and casteless society to be built up where every individual has full opportunity to grow according to his worth and ability. In particular, I hope that the curse of caste will be ended, for there cannot be either democracy or socialism on the basis of caste.

Four great religions have influenced India—two emerging from her own thought, Hinduism and Buddhism, and two coming from abroad but establishing themselves firmly in India, Christianity and Islam. Science today challenges the old concepts of religion. But if religion deals not with dogmas and ceremonials, but rather with the higher things of life, there should be no conflict with science or *inter se* between religions. It might be the high privilege of India to help in bringing about this synthesis. That would be in India's ancient tradition inscribed on Asoka's edicts.

Tomorrow's India will be what we make it by today's labours. We have started on this pilgrimage with strong purpose and good heart, and we shall reach the end of the journey, however long that might be.

What I am concerned with is not merely our material progress, but the quality and depth of our people. Gaining power through industrial processes, will they lose themselves in the quest of individual wealth and soft living? That would be a tragedy, for that would be a negation of what India has stood for in the past and, I hope, in the present time also as exemplified by Gandhiji. Can we combine the progress of science and technology with this progress of the mind and spirit also? We cannot be untrue to science, because that represents the basic fact of life today. Still less can we be untrue to those essential principles for which India has stood in the past throughout the ages.

✧ Waiting for the Mahatma ✧

R.K. Narayan

Mohandas Gandhi's reputation in India has never waned even though the nation's political course has taken directions he would have opposed, and scholars have interpreted and reinterpreted his contribution to Indian nationalism and the winning of independence. He is seen alternately as a saint, master political strategist, and utopian dreamer, but—in whatever guise—remains a figure of compelling interest in the Indian memory and imagination. A charismatic leader of such proportions is difficult to evaluate or analyze, and it is unlikely that historians and political scientists ever will succeed in mapping the true dimensions of his influence on India. It remains for the artists and creative writers to attempt to make an assessment. It is not unlikely that Gandhi will be transformed into a legend in the process, and the reader of this selection will be left to judge whether that transformation may not already be under way.

Several important novels have taken up the theme of Gandhi and his effect on India, including Raja Rao's *Kanthapura* (London: Allen & Unwin, 1938) and Mulk Raj Anand's *Untouchable* (Bombay: Jaico, 1956), but most attempt to portray Gandhi within a political context and thus lose something of the power of Gandhi's individual personality. R.K. Narayan's *Waiting for the Mahatma* (1955) avoids this problem by ignoring the major political events of the time.

Narayan (1906–2001) wrote in English and his novels were influenced by the leading writers of Britain and America. His content is uniquely Indian, however, blending tragedy and comedy without judging his characters. Most of his fourteen novels are set in a typical south India town in Mysore, which he has named Malgudi. *Waiting for the Mahatma* initially had a mixed reception, partly due to the unconventional characterization of Gandhi and partly because it appeared between his two most popular works, *The Financial Expert* (1953) and *The Guide* (1958). It is now considered one of his finest efforts.

Sriram, the hero of *Waiting for the Mahatma*, is an aimless youth living with his caustic grandmother. Granny had saved his father's monthly pension payments and turned the bank account over to him on his twentieth birthday. With no need to work for a living, he leads an indolent and passionless life until he meets Bharati, a young girl whose devotion to the Mahatma leaves her no time for romantic involvement. In order to be near her, Sriram joins the nationalist movement and finally wins her when Gandhi approves their union on the day of his death in 1948. Gandhi is seen through the eyes of this couple; he appears frequently throughout the book, but he is described primarily in his relations to the young couple. Other campaigners in the Indian independence movement and various people who attempt to exploit Gandhi for their own ends are included in the cast of characters. Gandhi becomes a multifaceted reflection of a few people with whom he has come in contact. Moreover, this approach allows Narayan to present a realistic view of the lives and concerns of a few common people living in uncommon times. The novel thus offers us a view of the last years of British rule in India that complements those of leaders such as Nehru and Gandhi himself.

In the following passage, Narayan portrays Sriram's conversion to Gandhi's movement, but leaves room for the reader to wonder what the young man's motivations truly are; perhaps he is not even sure himself. As the passage opens, the smitten Sriram has followed Bharati to a camp Gandhi has set up among the hovels of the untouchable city sweepers while on a visit to Malgudi. Sriram offers to join the movement, and Bharati tells him to return at three in the morning. When he does so, he unexpectedly finds himself face to face with Gandhi.

Questions

1. Does Sriram join with Gandhi exclusively because of his attraction to Bharati, or could he have other motives?
2. What does Sriram like and dislike about the life of Gandhi's volunteers?

3. How does Granny respond to Gandhi's campaign and to Sriram's intentions to take part in it?

Waiting for the Mahatma

R.K. Narayan, *Waiting for the Mahatma*
(East Lansing: Michigan State University Press, 1955),
pp. 55–60, 62–65, 70–72, 74–77

Granny had slept fitfully. She had gone up to Kanni's shop five times during the evening to enquire if anyone had seen Sriram, and sent a boy who had come to make a purchase there to look for Sriram everywhere. At last the schoolmaster who lived up the street told her as he passed her house,

"Your pet is in Mahatma's camp. I saw him."

"Ah! What was he doing there?" asked Granny, alarmed. For her the Mahatma was one who preached dangerously, who tried to bring untouchables into the temples, and who involved people in difficulties with the police. She didn't like the idea. She wailed, "Oh, master, why did you allow him to stay on there? You should have brought him away. It is so late and he has not come home. As his old teacher you should have weaned him away."

"Don't worry, madam, he is perfectly safe. How many of us could have the privilege of being so near the Mahatma? You must be happy that he is doing so well! Our country needs more young men like him."

Granny replied, "It is teachers like you who have ruined our boys and this country," and turned in, slamming the door.

He stood at the entrance to Mahatmaji's hut, holding his breath. It was very difficult to decide what he should do now. She had asked him to be present at the portals of the Great Presence, but perhaps she had been fooling him.

The door of Mahatmaji's hut was half open. Light streamed out through the gap. Sriram went towards it like a charmed moth. If he had paused to reflect he would not have believed himself to be capable of repeating a foolhardy act a second time. But through lack of sleep, and tension of nerves, a general recklessness had come over him, the same innocent charge that had taken him tumbling into the hut the previous evening took him there again now. He peeped in like a clown. The door was half open; he had over-estimated its width from a distance, for he could not peep in without thrusting his head through.

"Oh, there he is!" cried Bharati, with laughter in her voice. "You may open the door if you wish to come in," she said. Sriram felt again that the girl was making fun of him. Even in the great presence, she didn't seem to care. Here at least Sriram had hoped she would speak without the undertone of mischief. He felt so irritated at the thought that he replied with all the pungency he could muster in his tone: "You have—I waited for you there—"

"Come in, come in," said the Mahatma. "Why should you be standing there? You could have come straight in."

"But she asked me to wait outside," said Sriram, stepping in gingerly. From the door to where the Mahatma sat the distance was less than ten feet, but he felt he was taking hours to cover it. His legs felt weak and seemed to intertwine, he seemed to be walking like a drunkard, a particularly dangerous impression to create in the Mahatma, who was out to persuade even the scavengers to give up drinking. In a flash it occurred to him that he ought to have a sensible answer ready if the Mahatma should suddenly turn round and ask, "Have you been drinking toddy or whisky?"

But his trial came to an end, when Gandhi said, "Bharati has just been mentioning you." He spoke while his hands were busy turning a spinning wheel, drawing out a fine thread. A man sitting in a corner, with a pad resting on his knee, was writing. Mahatmaji himself as always was doing several things at the same time. While his hands were spinning, his eyes perused a letter held before him by another, and he found it possible too to put in a word of welcome to Sriram. Through the back door of the hut many others were coming in and passing out. For each one of them Mahatmaji had something to say.

He looked up at Sriram and said: "Sit down, young man. Come and sit as near me as you like." There was so much unaffected graciousness in his tone that Sriram lost all fear and hesitation. He moved briskly up. He sat on the floor near Mahatmaji and watched with fascination the smooth turning of the spinning wheel. Bharati went to an inner part of the hut, threw a swift look at Sriram, which he understood to mean, "Remember not to make a fool of yourself."

The Mahatma said, "Nowadays I generally get up an hour earlier in order to be able to do this: spinning a certain length is my most important work: even my prayer comes only after that. I'd very much like you to take a vow to wear only cloth made out of your own hands each day."

"Yes, I will do so," promised Sriram.

When the gong in the Taluk Office struck four, the Mahatma invited Sriram to go out with him for a walk.

During the last fifteen minutes of this walk the Mahatma said nothing; he walked in silence, looking at the ground before him. When the Mahatma was silent the others were even more so, the only movement they performed was putting one foot before another on the sand, keeping pace with him: some were panting hard and trying hard to suppress the sound. The Mahatma's silence was heavy and pervasive, and Sriram was afraid even to gulp or cough, although he very much wanted to clear his throat, cough, sneeze, swing his arms about. The only sound at the moment was the flowing of the river and the twitter of birds. Somewhere a cow was mooing. Even Bharati, the embodiment of frivolity, seemed to have become sombre. The Mahatma pulled out his watch, looked at it briefly and said, "We will go back, that is all the walk I can afford today." Sriram wanted to ask, "Why?" But he held his tongue. The Mahatma turned to him as they were walking back, "You have a grandmother, I hear, but no parents."

"Yes. My grandmother is very old."

"Yes, she must be, otherwise how can you call her a grandmother?" People laughed, Sriram too joined in this laughter out of politeness.

"Does she not miss you very much when you are away for so long?"

"Yes, very much. She gets very angry with me. I don't know what to do about it," said Sriram courageously rushing ahead. He felt pleased at having said something of his own accord, but his only fear was that Bharati might step in and say something nasty and embarrassing, but he was happy to note that Bharati kept her peace.

Mahatmaji said: "You must look after your granny too, she must have devoted herself to bringing you up."

"Yes, but when I am away like this she is very much upset."

"Is it necessary for you to be away from her so much?"

"Yes, Bapu, otherwise how can I do anything in this world?"

"What exactly do you want to do?"

It was now that Sriram became incoherent. He was seized with a rush of ideas and with all the confusion that too many ideas create. He said something, and the Mahatma watched him patiently, the others too held their breath and watched, and after a few moments of struggle for self-expression, Sriram was able to form a cogent sentence. It was the unrelenting pressure of his subconscious desires that jerked the sentence out of his lips, and he said, "I like to be where Bharati is." The Mahatma said, "Oh, is that so!" He patted Bharati's back and said, "What a fine friend you have! You must be pleased to have such a devoted friend. How long have you known him?"

Bharati said like a shot, "Since yesterday. I saw him for the first time sitting in your hut and I asked him who he was."

Sriram interposed and added, "But I knew her before, although I spoke to her only yesterday."

The Mahatma passed into his hut, and went on to attend to other things. Many people were waiting for him. Bharati disappeared into the Mahatma's hut the moment they arrived. Sriram fell back and got mixed up with a crowd waiting outside. He felt jealous of Bharati's position. She sought him out later and said, "You are probably unused to it, but in Bapu's presence we speak only the absolute truth and nothing less than that, and nothing more than that either."

He took her to task: "What will he think of me now when he knows that I have not known you long enough and yet—"

"Well, what?" she twitted him.

"And yet I wish to be with you and so on."

"Why don't you go in and tell him you have been speaking nonsense and that you were blurting out things without forethought or self-control? Why couldn't you have told him that you want to serve the country, that you are a patriot, that you want to shed your blood in order to see that the British leave the country? That is what most people say when they come near the Mahatma. I have seen hundreds of people come to him, and say the same thing."

"And he believes all that?" asked Sriram.

"Perhaps not, but he thinks it is not right to disbelieve anyone."

"But you say we must only speak the truth in his presence."

"If you can, of course, but if you can't, the best thing to do is maintain silence."

"Why are you so angry with me, is it not a part of your duty not to be angry with others?" asked Sriram pathetically.

"I don't care," said Bharati, "this is enough to irritate even the Mahatma. Now what will he think of me if he realizes I am encouraging a fellow like you to hang about the place, a fellow whom I have not known even for a full day yet!"

Sriram became reckless, and said breezily, "What does it matter how long I have known you? Did you think I was going to lie to him if you had not spoken before I spoke?"

These bickerings were brought to an end by someone calling "Bharati" from another hut. Bharati abandoned him and disappeared from the spot.

Bharati's words gave him an idea. He realized his own omission, and proposed to remedy it next time he walked with the Mahatma. Sriram's anxiety lest he fall asleep when the Mahatma was up kept him awake the whole night. He shared the space on the floor with one of the men in the camp. It was a strange feeling to lie down in a hut, and he felt he was becoming a citizen of an entirely new world. He missed the cosy room of his house in Kabir Lane, he missed the two pillows and the soft mattress and the carpet under it; even the street noises of Kabir Street added much to the domestic quality of life, and he missed it badly now. He had to adopt an entirely new mode of life. He had to live, of his own choice, in a narrow hut, with thatch above, with a dingy, sooty smell hanging about everything. The floor had been swept with cow dung and covered with a thin layer of sand. He had to snuggle his head on the crook of his arm for a pillow.

[Sriram spends a day in the camp and learns of the volunteers' commitment to poverty, nonviolence, self-suffering, and Indian independence, after which he feels ready to speak to Gandhi again.]

Sriram was told that he could accompany Mahatmaji in his tour of the villages on condition that he went home, and secured Granny's approval. Sriram tried to slur the matter over, he said it would not be necessary, he hinted he was an independent man used to such outings from home. The Mahatma's memory was better than that. He said with a smile, "I remember you said that she didn't like to see you mixing with us."

Sriram thought it over and said, "Yes, master, but how can I for ever remain tied to her? It is not possible."

"Are you quite sure that you want to change your style of life?" asked the Mahatma.

"I can think of nothing else," Sriram said. "How can I live as I have lived all these years?" He threw a quick glance at Bharati as she came in with some letters for the Mahatma. Her look prevented him from completing the sentence, which would have run, "And I always wish to be with Bharati and not with my grandmother."

The Mahatma said, "I shall be happy to have you with us as long as you like, but you must first go home and tell your grandmother and receive her blessing. You must tell her frankly what you wish to do, but you must cause her no pain."

Sriram hesitated. The prospect of facing Granny was unnerving. The thought of her was like the thought of an unreal troublesome world, one which he hoped he had left behind for ever: the real world for him now was the one of Bharati, Gorpad, unslaughtered naturally dying animals, the Mahatma, spinning wheels. He wanted to be here all the time; it seemed impossible for him to go back to Kabir Street, that pyol, and that shop, and those people there who treated him as if he were only eight years old. He stood before the Mahatma as if to appeal to him not to press him to go and face his grandmother, but the master was unrelenting. "Go and speak to her. I don't think she is so unreasonable as to deny you your ambitions. Tell her that I would like to have you with me. If you tour with me the next two weeks, you will observe and learn much that may be useful to you later in life. Tell her she will feel glad that she let you go. Assure her that I will look after you safely." Every word filled him with dread when he remembered the terms in which Granny referred to the Mahatma. He dared not even give the slightest indication as to how she would react. He felt a great pity for the Mahatma, so innocent that he could not dream of anyone talking ill of him. He felt angry at the thought of Granny, such an ill-informed, ignorant and bigoted personality! What business had she to complicate his existence in this way? If he could have had his will he would have ignored his grandmother, but he had to obey the Mahatma now.

He said, "All right, sir. I will go and get my granny's blessing. I'll be back early tomorrow."

[He summons up his courage and returns home. Apparently made anxious by his absence, Granny feeds him delicacies and ridicules the lifestyle of the volunteers.]

Sriram was horrified. "What do you take the Mahatma for! Do you know, he won't even wear sandals made of the hide of slaughtered animals!"

Granny was seized by a fit of laughter. Tears rolled down her cheeks. "Won't wear sandals!" she cried in uncontrollable laughter. "Never heard of such a thing before! How do they manage it? By peeling off the skin of animals before they are slaughtered, is that it?"

"Shut up, Granny!" cried Sriram in a great rage. "What an irresponsible gossip you are! I never thought you could be so bad!"

Granny for the first time noticed a fiery earnestness in her grandson, and gathered herself up. She said: "Oh! He is your God, is he?"

"Yes, he is, and I won't hear anyone speak lightly of him."

"What else can I know, a poor ignorant hag like me! Do I read the newspapers? Do I listen to lectures? Am I told what is what by anyone? How should I know anything about that man Gandhi!"

"He is not a man; he is a Mahatma!" cried Sriram.

"What do you know about a Mahatma, anyway?" asked Granny.

Sriram fidgeted and rocked himself in his chair in great anger. He had not come prepared to face a situation of this kind. He had been only prepared to face a granny who might show sullenness at his absence, create difficulties for him when he wanted to go away and exhibit more sorrow and rage than levity. But here she was absolutely reckless, frivolous, and without the slightest sense of responsibility or respect. This was a situation which he had not anticipated, and he had no technique to meet it. It was no use, he realized, showing righteous indignation: that would only tickle the old lady more and more, and when the time came for him to take her permission and go, she might become too intractable.

Granny came back to her original mood after all these unexpected transitions. She said: "You must eat your dinner, my boy," very earnestly. She bustled about again as if for a distinguished visitor. She pulled a dining leaf out of a bundle in the kitchen rack, spread it on the floor, sprinkled a little water on it, and drew the bronze rice pot nearer, and sat down in order to be able to serve him without getting up again. The little lamp wavered in its holder. He ate in silence, took a drink of water out of the good old brass tumbler that was by his side; he cast a glance at the old bronze vessel out of which rice had been served to him for years. He suddenly felt depressed at the sight of it all. He was oppressed with the thought that he was leaving these old associations, that this was really a farewell party. He was going into an unknown life right from here. God knew what was in store for him. He felt very gloomy at the thought of it all. He knew it would be no good ever talking to his granny about his plans, or the Mahatma or Bharati. All that was completely beyond her comprehension. She would understand only edibles and dinner and fasting at night in order to impress a neighbour with her austerity. No use talking to her about anything. Best to leave in the morning without any fuss. He had obeyed Mahatmaji's mandate to the extent of seeing her and speaking to her. The Mahatma should be satisfied and not expect him to be able to bring about a conversion in the old lady's outlook, enough to earn her blessing.

Granny was very old, probably eighty, ninety, or a hundred. He had never tried to ascertain her age correctly. And she would not understand new things. At dead of night, after assuring himself that Granny was fast asleep, he got up, scribbled a note to her by the night lamp, and placed it under the brass pot containing water on the window sill, which she was bound to lift first thing in the morning. She could carry it to a neighbour and have it read to her if she had any difficulty in finding her glasses. Perhaps she might not like to have it read by the neighbours. She would always cry: "Sriram, my glasses, where are the wretched glasses gone?" whenever anything came to her hand for reading, and it would be his duty to go to the cupboard, and fetch them. Now he performed the same duty in anticipation. He tip-toed to the almirah, took the glasses out of their case silently, and returned to the hall, leaving the spectacle case open, because it had a tendency to close with a loud clap. He placed the glasses beside his letter of farewell, silently opened the door, and stepped into the night.

✧ All Is Burning ✧

Jean Arasanayagam

The decline and fall of the Soviet Union from 1985 to 1991 led many people to hope that tragic Cold War mistakes such as the U.S. war in Vietnam and the USSR's war in Afghanistan would be avoided in the future. In fact, political violence has increased as internecine rivalries that had been suppressed by the Cold War added to ongoing civil conflicts. Violence has taken many forms. This short story describes one of the many innocent victims in this period.

Some conflicts became global as large nations remade power relationships and institutions in the post–Cold War era—for example, Kosovo, Bosnia, Rwanda, Sudan, Afghanistan, and Iraq. Even localized civil wars, such as those in Sri Lanka, involved international actors. Insurgents engage in the illegal arms trade, extortion of money from overseas supporters, and legal and illegal business enterprises to finance their warfare. Governments hire mercenaries, train counterinsurgent forces overseas, and lobby the major powers for support. In Sri Lanka, India sent an army (Indian Peace-Keeping Force or IPKF) in the 1980s; Norway and other nations provided humanitarian services and political mediators. Hundreds of non-governmental organizations (NGOs) sent representatives.

Villagers such as Alice in this story cared little for these developments but felt the full impact of them, often in the form of terrorism from both sides. Terrorism is an ancient tactic intended to destroy the enemy through violence against the people. In a civil war, each side intends to deter support for the other by convincing people that its wrath is greater than its opponent's. Sometimes the violence is selective, assassinating leaders of the opponents; increasingly it has become indiscriminate violence against entire communities, as in this story.

This short story, from a collection of the same name, could have been set in many parts of the world, but is set in a particular moment in Sri Lankan history. Since it gained its independence from Britain in 1948, Sri Lanka had been ruled by two parties representing factions in the Sinhalese elite. Neither party was able to create a stable and prosperous society. The economy declined, unemployment rose, and tension between the majority Sinhalese and the Tamil minority increased. In 1970 Sirima Bandaranaike was swept into power on a platform of radical socialist changes, inspired in part by her infatuation with Maoist China. The economy declined further and the Janatha Vimukthi Peramuna (JVP) party opposed the government for not being radical enough. After an abortive attempt at an uprising in April 1971, the JVP leaders were imprisoned but later released.

Sri Lanka faced much greater disasters after 1971. Bandaranaike implemented a new constitution and administrative reforms to placate rebellious Sinhalese youth and Buddhist leaders. Relations between the majority Sinhalese and the minority Tamils worsened in the 1970s—in part because of these measures. The leading Tamil political party declared that it intended to create a separate Tamil state. This movement was taken over by revolutionaries, and the nation broke out in a civil war that continued until May 2009, with many atrocities on both sides.

In 1977 a new government was elected that gave itself near-dictatorial powers in order to impose an export-oriented "open economy." It also used emergency laws and extralegal measures to carry out arbitrary and retaliatory torture and killings of Tamil civilians as the separatists gained in power. In 1987 the IPKF arrived in the country to force a settlement to the ethnic conflict, but ended up fighting the Tamil separatists itself.

The JVP, reviving in the guise of a radical Sinhalese Buddhist nationalist movement, seized power in many of the Sinhalese majority areas, enforced by terrorism. It mobilized frustrated Sinhalese youth, politicians out of power, and Buddhist fundamentalists against the economic changes, the dictatorial government, and the presence of the IPKF. The JVP killed up to 17,000 people; in the brutal suppression of the JVP, the government, and vigilantes acting in its behalf, killed up to 23,000 people. "All Is Burning" takes place in this period from 1987 to 1990.

Jean Arasanayagam was born into one of Sri Lanka's minority communities, the "Dutch Burghers," descendants of the colonial rulers in the seventeenth and eighteenth centuries. She married into another minority community, the Tamils—her poetry expresses the sorrow of being ostracized by her husband's family, who opposed the marriage. Jean Arasanayagam is best known as a poet; much of her poetry in the 1980s dealt with the civil war.

Ironically, Alice, Seela, and Seela's fiancé Sena are from the Sinhalese Buddhist community that both the JVP and the government claimed to represent. The title refers to a famous sermon attributed to the Buddha, the Fire Sermon. In it, the Buddha says that the senses, and the contact they make with the world, are burning. The Buddha urges people to become dispassionate, to restrain these fires so that they no longer have hold. In the end, Buddhism sustains Alice through this horrible experience.

Many websites dealing with civil war and terrorism in Sri Lanka are highly partisan accounts. One well-illustrated source of information is the Peace and Conflict Timeline of the Centre for Poverty Analysis at http://pact.lk.

Questions

1. Is Alice's behavior consistent with the teachings of the Buddha as presented in earlier readings? Why does she say that being called "mother" by the dying youth "is enough"?
2. Is the suffering of ordinary people inevitable in times of radical change? How could this kind of tragedy be avoided, if at all? What sort of political leadership is needed to make the modest goals of a person like Alice attainable?
3. Yama is considered a Hindu deity, but he is real to Alice. Is this a sign of religious syncretism in popular religion in South Asia comparable to the literary syncretism in earlier readings?

All Is Burning

Jean Arasanayagam, "All Is Burning," in *All Is Burning* (New Delhi: Penguin, 1995), 166–176

Bhikkus, all is burning. And what is the all that is burning? Bhikkus, the eye is burning, visible forms are burning, visual consciousness is burning, visual impression is burning. . . . Burning with what? Burning with the fire of lust, with the fire of hate, with the fire of delusion; I say it is burning with birth, ageing and death, with sorrows, with lamentations, with pains, with griefs, with despairs.

—The Buddha's Fire Sermon

SHE BLEW OUT the flame of the bottle lamp, leaving the room in darkness. She took a towel off the line and wrapped it about her shoulders. Seela, her daughter, a young woman in her twenties, sat at the table with her head in her hands.

Night sounds filtered in through the clay walls of the hut. Not just the sounds of insects rasping against the leaves or of wakened birds, but also a vast sighing that rippled through the thick blue-black shadows that lay like welts on the earth.

Seela lifted her head wearily. The weight of melancholy, of despair pressed each image onto her consciousness. She had aged. Felt older than her mother. In the cavern of her being images of dead fish, silver bellies upturned, floated in an inky pool.

"Mother," she whispered. "Mother, shall we go in search of Sena? He may still be alive if he has not been taken away. I'll come with you. You can't go alone. They may still be there, who knows. We can guide each other. It's still not light, we have to search for the path. It may be an unfamiliar one."

Alice was already at the door. She spoke under her breath. "No, you wait. Don't open the door to anyone. Remain in darkness. Don't light the lamp."

"Mother."

"Yes?"

"Don't go alone." Seela rose wearily and dragged her feet to the door.

"No. It is my mission. A journey by myself will be safer. I'll come back here. Don't move. Wait and keep that door barred. Just don't open to any knock."

Alice stepped out, treading softly, warily on her bare feet. It would be easier that way. No sound of any footfall. She closed the door behind her very quietly. She peered into the darkness with yet its hint of light. Her nerves felt on edge. Her instincts alert, she must let herself be guided, by odours—unusual odours of gunshot, of blood, borne by the slight, chill tremors of wind. There would be that human odour too, of fear, that rank smell of bodies through whose pores fear had breathed.

The sky began to lighten very faintly. Pale innocent streaks of colour appeared before the darker, reddened contusions that bruised the clouds. She walked along in a half-blind, almost groping way, feeling the roughness of tussocks of grass and dislodged stones that trembled beneath her feet.

She still felt her flesh raw, hurt by the events of the night. That sense of peace which came with late evening and the dusk which settled over the river, the trees, the road and their little hamlet had been deceptive. The bathers had returned from the river, they did not linger very long these days. The water, silver shot with ripples of gold, soon turned dark and opaque, vanishing into the dense clumps of trees. The woodsmoke curled up from the huts, spiralling into the sky, a pale wreathing grey.

She had been busy preparing the evening meal. The pot of rice was still on the fire, the fish and vegetables simmering in their pots. Seela, her daughter, was talking to Sena, the young man whom she was going to marry. Alice wanted this marriage for Seela. Her own man had deserted her when she was pregnant, leaving her to bring up the child alone. She had been a servant in so many houses, cooking, minding children, washing piles of linen, dressing her child in the clothes outgrown by other people's children—her mistress's daughter's clothes and those of her friends' children. No more of that for Seela. She had been a bright, intelligent child, had gone to school, passed examinations. She had a future before her. All that was through the efforts, undoubtedly, that Alice had made.

But it had come to their hamlet too—the *bhishanaya*, the trouble. Yes, it had reached them. There were rumours. The young men in the village, were they too involved in all those happenings? The country was on fire. Everything was on fire. All was burning, burning. Yes, the fires were burning. Fires that burnt down the huts. These and hundreds of other villages burning. The self burning. The unconscious, the visual impressions, burning. The fire of lust and hate, the fire of delusion. The Buddha's Fire Sermon that the villagers heard in the temple—the monk repeated it on the last poya [full-moon] day when they went to hear him, to find some relief for their suffering minds.

"Burning," he said, "with birth, ageing and death, with sorrows, with lamentations, with pains, with griefs, with despairs."

And what do we do? Alice thought to herself. Become dispassionate, detached? To reach that liberation must I first go out among the dead and their ruined houses? I cannot forget the sound of the vehicles on the road. . . .

They had stopped at the entrance to the village. The darkness had moved like an open door to admit them. And they had entered. The villagers heard the sounds of their boots. The knocking at the doors. The commands.

"Open up."

There was nothing else to do.

Screams. Dying away. Growing fainter. Fainter. She had to go. But not at once. Wait for some time. Till they heard the sound of the vehicles moving off. Then she would go out, in search of Sena, for Seela's sake. She thought of herself. An ordinary woman. Very ordinary. Even the name Alice did not matter to anyone. She knew that she had to do it. Even if there were a vestige of life left she would confront those last moments. And she would have to do it alone.

Seela too had been strong during those last moments. "Mother, our generation, my generation, we know the consequences. We are not afraid."

Now Alice was walking along pathways. They had to lead to the death-spot. Through the grove of trees—wild guava, hard-shelled green belly fruit and straggling palms. A cluster of thambili [king coconuts] nestled among some of the thicker fronds, a very pale orange. Her throat felt parched, as if death were already clutching at it. Dry tongued, her belly cavernous and hollow. Out of the trees, out of the grove, she emerged like a sleepwalker into a space where the grass had been trampled and crushed.

Now it was over. The sound of gunshot still echoed in her ears. Yama had visited every house in the village where there were males. They had all been taken away. She had to summon all her strength for this mission. The vision of Yama, the god of death, filled her mind.

I am an ordinary woman, she told herself. I have been a servant in other people's homes for the greater part of my life. Always subservient, obeying orders. Eating after everyone else had eaten. Sleeping on my mat in a corner of a room, seeing that other people were comfortable. And now, now that I had hopes for a different kind of life, now when I thought things would change—but no, things have changed, though not for the better. Yet I have to do this for my daughter, look at the faces of the dead and dying. No, Seela couldn't do it. I'll do it for her. I am her mother. Who else has she had all her life? Myself and her grandmother. Two women. There has never been a man to give me strength. I have done things that I never believed possible for a woman to do.

No, it will never end for me. My strength grows with each crisis. I've been well trained through the years. There's no one else I can turn to. I'll do it by myself. I can't help it if my mind keeps going back to all the events of the night. I'll relive this experience for ever.

The knocking on all those doors resounded in her ears. She had opened the door. What else could she have done? They wanted Sena. As they did all the males in the village. Behind them she saw that vision—Yama. Yama, the god of death. He too was with them. On whose side was he? He was a constant guest on both fronts these days.

They pointed the guns at Sena. No, he couldn't escape. Nor could all the others. Weeping, shrieking echoed through the night, the night that Alice had thought would be so peaceful. She smelt burning rice. The brands crackled and the fire raced, shedding sparks as it blew up.

Yama, Yama. Was it only she who saw him? Eye for an eye, tooth for a tooth, the men kept saying as they pointed the gun at Sena, prodded him with the butt.

"Don't try to resist," said one of them. "And don't say you are innocent. You want to be martyrs. Then where are the victims? Someone has to be the victim. Who put up all those posters with their violent messages? Who carried off the weapons after the attacks on police stations and the army camps? To use for what purpose? To use against whom? The men of this village—we have proof. The last attack . . . there were deaths. Now get on, move on. . . . The fires are spreading all over the country. Come on, hurry up."

Her daughter had fallen at the feet of the men. She had pleaded and wept.

"Don't take him away. Don't. Don't." It had all fallen on deaf ears.

There had been so much shouting outside their walls. Commands. Tramp of boots. Sounds of running feet. They had heard the guns. The volley of shots. Went on ceaselessly. Would they ever stop firing?

It seemed a lifetime ago. Alice now smelt the odour of death. Rank. Foetid. Like rotting vegetation. They lay there, clumps of them, their bodies spreadeagled on the earth. Men. Bodies. A mirror of light flickered across her gaze with their distortions, black specks, rust coloured streaks—chiaroscuric images that almost stoned her eyeballs.

She knew she had to go among them. How else would she find Sena? He had to be there. He had to, unless . . . but could he have had a chance of escaping, in the dark? No, there must have been flashlights. The darkness violated by those coruscating beams. At least if she could find him. . . . She was a woman who needed certainty. The certainty of truth. It had to be one way or the other. She had never deceived Seela. Nor had she deceived herself. At this moment she did not want the comfort of any human being. This would be her final test, her trial. And Sena, if he still had some life in him, even if he was barely breathing, perhaps he could gasp out a word, perhaps she could even drag him out of this welter of bodies.

She looked at them, almost dispassionately. They were finished. There was nothing more left for them. Their women would have to fend for themselves now. The women were strong enough. And they had their children. They couldn't give up at this stage.

She wiped her face with the edge of her towel. The towel was damp with morning dew. Her face chill and sharp like the edge of a keen blade.

Death walk. That's what this is, she thought. I'll have to turn them over. I have to see the faces. How else can I recognize them? How can I recognize Sena? Men who had belonged to other women. I would never have touched them at any other time.

Her bare feet slid cautiously through the huddle of bodies. They felt so soft. Even the sinewy ones.

She bent over, turned up face after face. All she recognized were the empty faces of men. Men who were all akin, all brothers, husbands, fathers. All gone. To leave life in so unfinished, so haphazard a manner.

She stumbled, almost fell against one of the bodies. I'll have to be careful, she thought. I mustn't jostle them even in death. Perhaps, some of them still have that last breath . . . the soul that's reluctant to leave the body. No funeral orations for any of them. Individual burials are no longer practicable. It is within our minds that we carry those reminders of what each man was to each woman. Till each one is claimed, if ever they are claimed, they are anonymous. It's happening elsewhere too, perhaps at this very moment. . . . Soon there'll be no birds left in the village. Startled by gunshot, they'll fly away to another village. Who's going to start life here all over again . . .

Her movements now became mechanical. But she wove her way through, a searcher who could never give up the search.

Where would the pyres be lit? And where the secret graves? They would be silently carried away, secretly buried. Their names would be mentioned only in whispers. So this was the journey that Yama took daily? Difficult. But she had the strength.

She flicked at a fly with a towel. They were already there, the bluebottles. The smell of death, it was choking her. She felt suffocated but could not stop. She would go on till she found him.

Could this be Sena . . . ? She peered into a face, called his name softly: "Sena, Sena, Sena." It could be Sena—a young body, but the face all smeared with blood. If she wiped the blood off she might recognize him. She wiped his face gently with the end of her towel and gazed into the face.

No, this was not him. Resembled him . . .

She stroked his head, caressingly. A woman's gesture. Her towel was sodden. Her clothes felt damp.

He is still warm, she told herself. My towel is soaked with blood. My clothes too . . . damp, stained. She felt dead, her limbs numbed. She stumbled against yet another body.

There must be so many . . . so many of them. . . . Forgive me, she whispered softly. . . . Respect for the dead, incantations, prayers . . . I can't forget it. Forgive me, son, brother, father, husband, forgive me for touching your sleeping body with my foot, it is not that I mean to insult you . . .

No, not this one either. Where was he? And such a silence in the village. Where was everybody? Asleep? Awake? Afraid to come out? All the women, the children? Such a silence in the village.

Her head was full of images, strange thoughts. . . . All the blood must seep into the earth, as if the gods must be propitiated, as if we have had a long drought. What new plants will grow here? Or will it remain a desert, haunted by ghosts and spirits? Shouldn't we leave it this way, to remember them? I must go down to the river, wash my clothes, bathe, watch the water change colour—like my dreams, the dreams that will visit me night after night.

When can I ever complete this journey? Yama told me—somewhere—that this is my first journey into the darkness of the underworld. . . . What's that sound . . . a groan? Not all are dead then.

She knelt down. Her back ached with so much bending. She felt the man's breath touch the palm of her hand like a slight vapour, a cobweb of mist that faintly wreathed round her fingers.

"I won't leave you alone. I'll stay by you," she said, sitting beside him, wiping his face with the corner of her towel, pushing away the tangled strands of hair from his forehead. She supported his head in her arms.

"Mother," he uttered faintly. His life was ebbing away.

"Mother," he repeated. "Thirsty."

"Wait, I'll bring you a sip of water. I'll go back to my hut. Wait. Don't move."

No, there wasn't time to go back, to fetch water, to give him that drink. Life-giving water? No. It would soon be over. She felt the spasms of his chest, the painful heaving of that wounded breast. She held him until he was still. Her hands were stained with blood. She wiped them slowly but the blood felt sticky, oozing into her skin, her flesh.

That was the end. All she could give him was the hope of that sip of water. And he had called her Mother. That was enough. She was a comfort to him and that was more than all the others had on all the battlefields where they gasped out their lives.

Already, so many bodies and she hadn't found Sena yet.

What could a village do without all its men? We'll have to take their place now, we women, she thought. I'll go back to my daughter. Perhaps there's still hope. They may have taken him away for questioning. Seela will have to continue living, like all the other women. It won't be the end for us, not while we still have breath.

She rose wearily. She wanted to retch but her mouth was dry, her throat parched.

Two hundred and fifty of them. All the men in the village. Gone. Swept away in that great flood of death. But the women would bear more sons. Life had to, would go on.

Reflection

The great cultural achievements of South Asia in literature, art, architecture, and the history of its civilization continue to be respected and lovingly preserved. One of the great contributions of South Asia to the modern world is its demonstration that various approaches to life are possible in an industrial and postindustrial world. It is not necessary that impersonal economic forces and the requirements of technological progress create a uniform and faceless world society. In the complex and diverse world of the future, it will be necessary for every people to understand and appreciate what the others have to offer.

Bibliography

The editor wishes to thank the publishers and copyright holders for permission to reprint the preceding selections, which are listed below in order of their appearance.

VEDIC HYMNS from Ralph T.H. Griffith, trans., *Hymns of the Rigveda* (Benares: E.J. Lazarus, 1897).

SERMON AT THE DEER PARK from Paul Carus, *The Gospel of Buddha*, According to Old Records, 4th revised ed. (Chicago: Open Court Publishing, 1896), pp. 30–33, 37–43.

BHAGAVAD GITA from Edwin Arnold, trans., *The Song Celestial; or Bhagavad-gītā (from the Mahābhārata) Being a Discourse between Arjuna, Prince of India, and the Supreme Being under the Form of Krishna* (Boston: Roberts Brothers, 1885.)

ARTHASASTRA from Rudrapatnam Shamasastry, trans., *Kautilya's Arthaśāstra* (Bangalore: Government Press, 1915), pp. 36–39, 287, 289–296.

POEMS OF LOVE AND WAR from A.K. Ramanujan, sel. and trans., *Poems of Love and War from the Eight Anthologies and the Ten Long Poems of Classical Tamil* (New York: Columbia University Press, 1985), pp. 5, 16, 17, 22–23, 63, 115–117, 120, 123, 179, 218.

MAHĀVAMSA from Wilhelm Geiger, trans., *Mahāvamsa: The Great Chronicle of Ceylon* (Colombo: Ceylon Government Printer, 1912), pp. 143–144, 146, 149–151, 153–154, 170–171, 174–175, 177–178.

THE PERFECT BRIDE from J.A.B. van Buitenen, trans., *Tales of Ancient India* (Chicago: University of Chicago Press, 1959), pp. 157–160.

GITAGOVINDA from Edwin Arnold, *Poems* (Boston: Little, Brown, 1910), pp. 1–5, 9–14, 79–87.

SONGS OF KABIR from Rabindranath Tagore, trans., *Songs of Kabir* (New York: Macmillan, 1915), pp. 45–46, 56–57, 70–71, 75–76, 80–81, 112, 142–143.

SACRED WRITINGS OF THE SIKHS from Jodh Singh, Kapur Singh, Bawa Harkishen Singh, and Khushwant Singh, trans., *Sacred Writings of the Sikhs,* UNESCO Collection of Representative Works, Indian Series (London: Unwin Hyman, 1960)

AKBAR NAMA from Abu-l Fazl, *Akbar Nama*, trans., Henry Beveridge (Calcutta: Royal Asiatic Society, 1897), 364–367, 369–372.

HANUMAN CHALISA from "Appendix. Two Poems in Praise of Hanuman (Attributed to Tulsidas)," in Philip Lutgendorf, *Hanuman's Tale: The Messages of a Divine Monkey* (Oxford: Oxford University Press, 2007), pp. 397–399.

ON THE BURNING OF WIDOWS from Jogendra Chunder Ghose, ed., *The English Works of Raja Ram Mohan Roy*, vol. 1 (Calcutta: Srikanta Roy, 1901), pp. 123–128, 130–132, 134–138, 317–320.

GOVINDA SAMANTA from Lal Behari Day, *Govinda Samanta, or the History of a Bengal Raiyat* (London: Macmillan, 1874), pp. 69, 71–78, 112–117, 123–125.

GITANJALI from Rabindranath Tagore, *Gitanjali: Song Offerings* (London: Macmillan, 1913), pp. vii–xxii, 1–27.

HIND SWARAJ from "Hind Swaraj," in *Indian Home Rule by M.K. Gandhi. Being a translation of "Hind Swaraj" (Indian Home Rule), published in the Gujarati columns of* Indian Opinion, *11th and 18th December 1909* (Phoenix, Natal: International Printing Press, 1910), pp. 6–7, 14–15, 19–24, 36–37, 39, 47–50, 52–53, 61, 64.

MUNA AND MADAN from Michael James Hutt, trans. and ed., *Himalayan Voices: An Introduction to Modern Nepali Literature* (Berkeley: University of California Press, 1991), pp. 46–51.

WHAT IS INDIA? from Jawaharlal Nehru, "Synthesis Is Our Tradition," in Sarvepalli Gopal, ed., *Jawaharlal Nehru: An Anthology* (Oxford: Oxford University Press, 1980), pp. 225–230.

WAITING FOR THE MAHATMA from R.K. Narayan, *Waiting for the Mahatma* (East Lansing: Michigan State University Press, 1955), pp. 55–60, 62–65, 70–72, 74–77.

ALL IS BURNING from Jean Arasanayagam, "All Is Burning," in *All Is Burning* (New Delhi: Penguin, 1995), 166–176.

About the Editor

Patrick Peebles is Professor Emeritus in History at the University of Missouri at Kansas City, where he taught courses on Asian history. He is a specialist on the modern history of Sri Lanka. In 2008–2009, he carried out research in Sri Lanka under a grant from the American Institute for Sri Lankan Studies for a book on the transformation of the colony from a military outpost to a plantation economy in the period from 1833 to 1850. In the fall of 2009, he taught in London in the Missouri London Program. His most recent research and book project is his microhistory of the East India Company from 1680 to 1700. He is a contributor to a number of encyclopedias and dictionaries on South Asia, and his books include *History of Sri Lanka* (2006), *Plantation Tamils of Ceylon* (2001), *Social Change in Nineteenth Century Ceylon* (1995), and *Classics of Eastern Thought* (1994).

www.ingramcontent.com/pod-product-compliance
Ingram Content Group UK Ltd.
Pitfield, Milton Keynes, MK11 3LW, UK
UKHW021608240425
457818UK00018B/446